SCRIBBLES + DOODLES

❧ a Coloring Journal ❧

Papeterie Bleu

Illustrated by Amalie

ISBN-13: 978-1945888236
ISBN-10: 1945888237

This journal belongs to:

_____

_____

This journal will inspire you to color, write, doodle and dream. There are quotes to ponder & use as writing prompts, or let your own imagination take over and fill the blank space in any way that you wish!

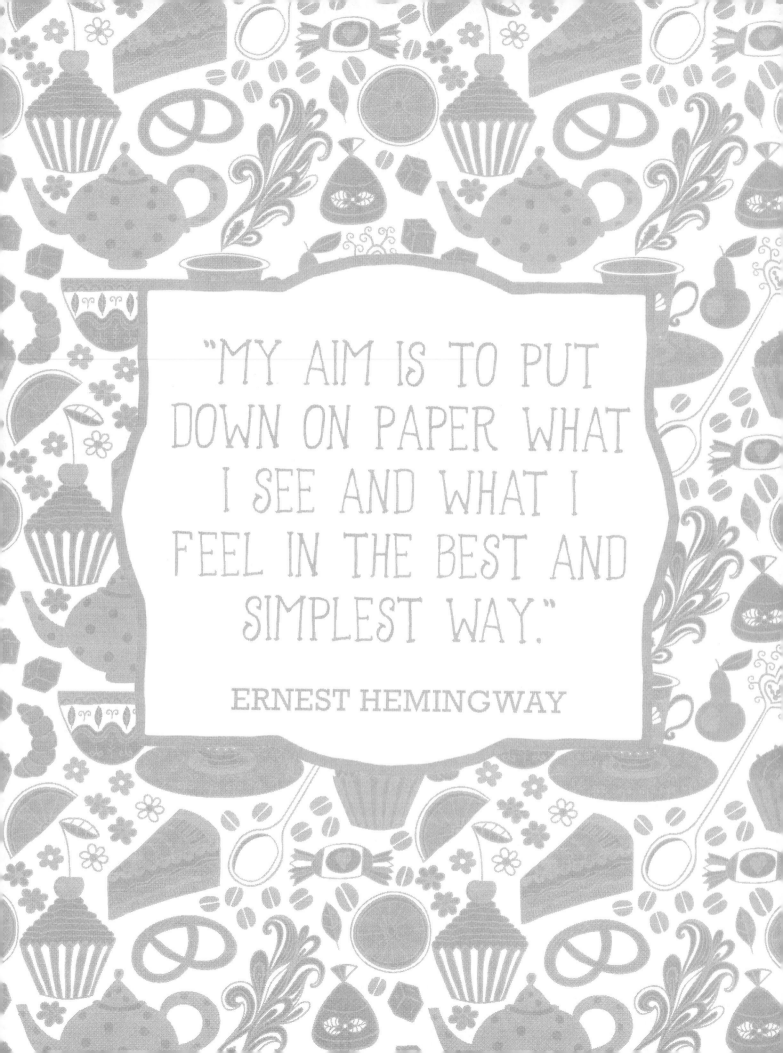

"MY AIM IS TO PUT DOWN ON PAPER WHAT I SEE AND WHAT I FEEL IN THE BEST AND SIMPLEST WAY."

ERNEST HEMINGWAY

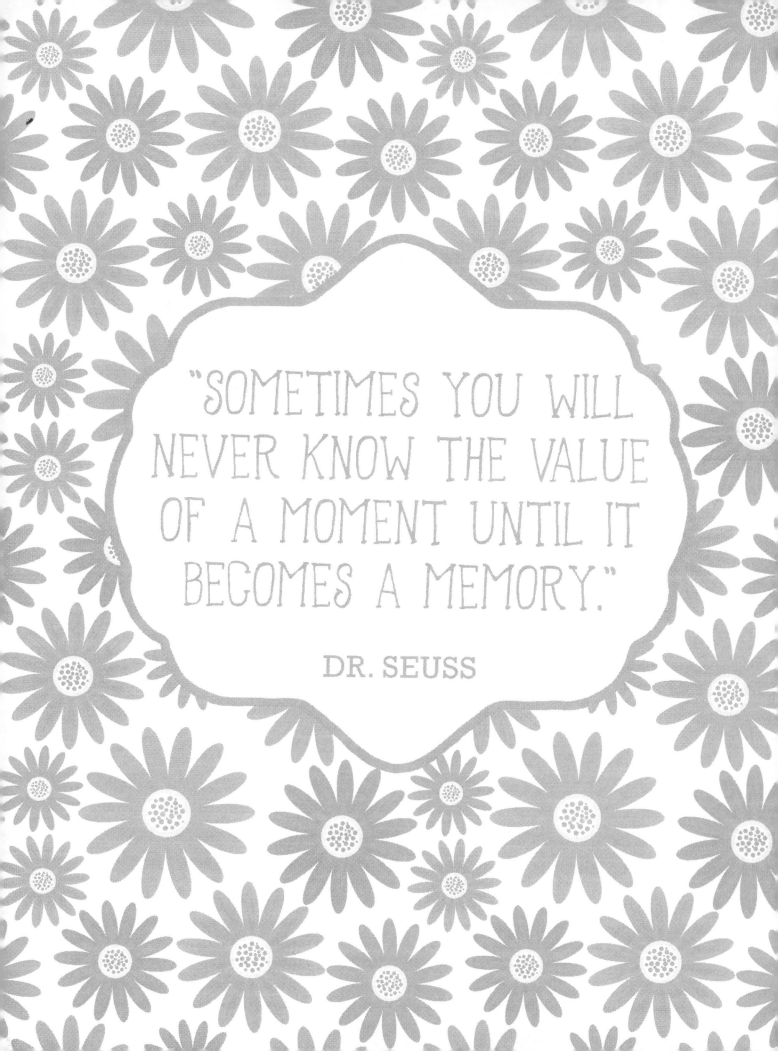

"SOMETIMES YOU WILL NEVER KNOW THE VALUE OF A MOMENT UNTIL IT BECOMES A MEMORY."

DR. SEUSS

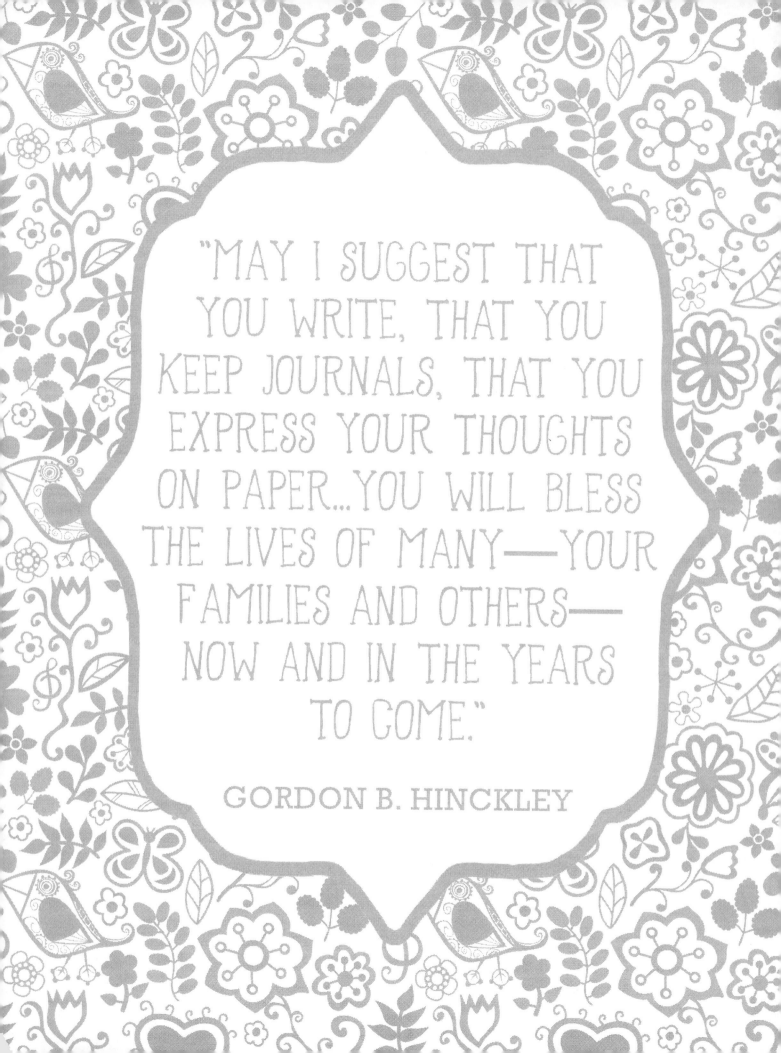

"MAY I SUGGEST THAT YOU WRITE, THAT YOU KEEP JOURNALS, THAT YOU EXPRESS YOUR THOUGHTS ON PAPER...YOU WILL BLESS THE LIVES OF MANY—YOUR FAMILIES AND OTHERS—NOW AND IN THE YEARS TO COME."

GORDON B. HINCKLEY

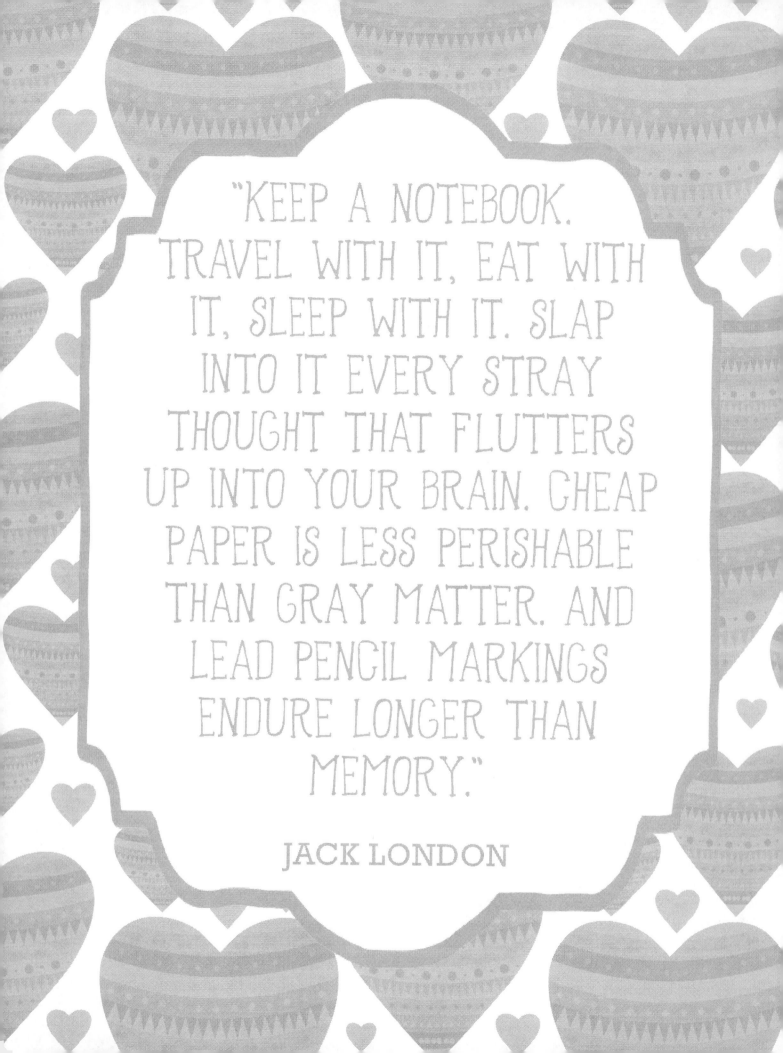

"KEEP A NOTEBOOK. TRAVEL WITH IT, EAT WITH IT, SLEEP WITH IT. SLAP INTO IT EVERY STRAY THOUGHT THAT FLUTTERS UP INTO YOUR BRAIN. CHEAP PAPER IS LESS PERISHABLE THAN GRAY MATTER. AND LEAD PENCIL MARKINGS ENDURE LONGER THAN MEMORY."

JACK LONDON

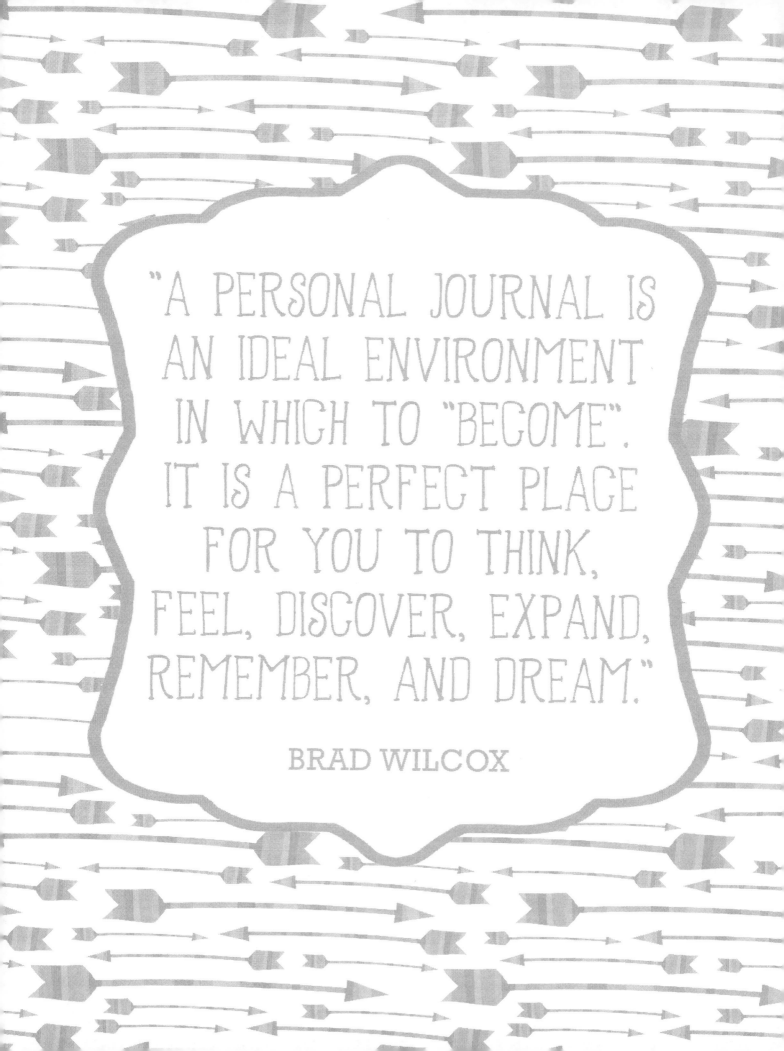

"A PERSONAL JOURNAL IS AN IDEAL ENVIRONMENT IN WHICH TO "BECOME". IT IS A PERFECT PLACE FOR YOU TO THINK, FEEL, DISCOVER, EXPAND, REMEMBER, AND DREAM."

BRAD WILCOX

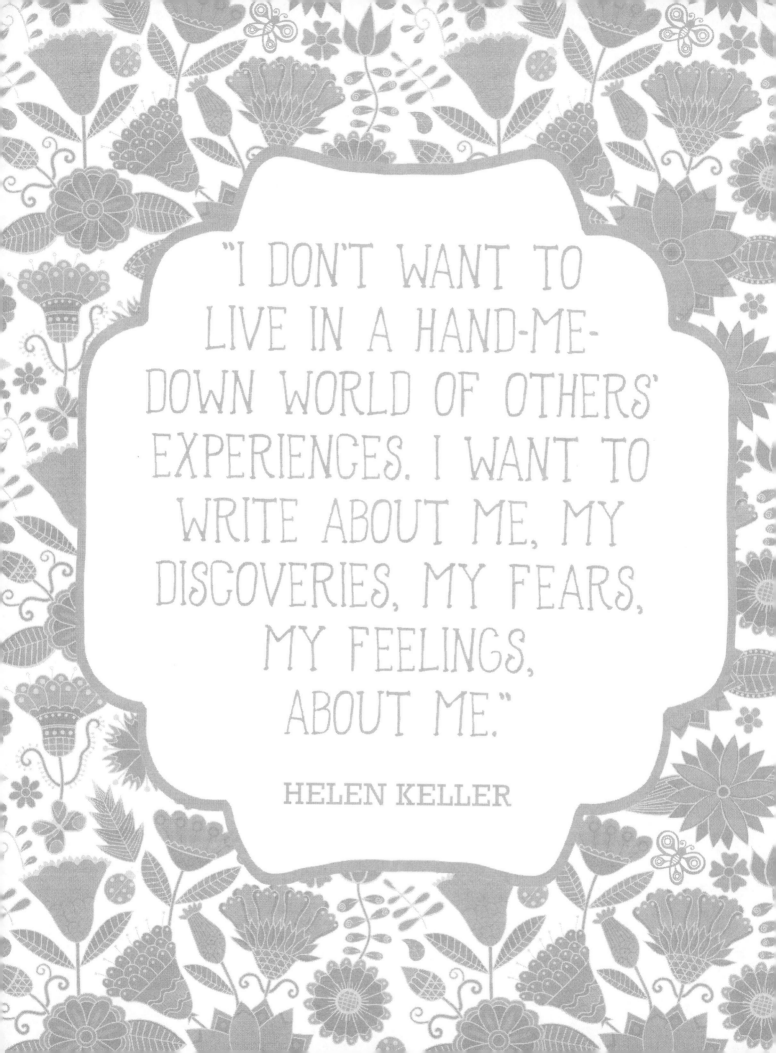

"I DON'T WANT TO LIVE IN A HAND-ME-DOWN WORLD OF OTHERS' EXPERIENCES. I WANT TO WRITE ABOUT ME, MY DISCOVERIES, MY FEARS, MY FEELINGS, ABOUT ME."

HELEN KELLER

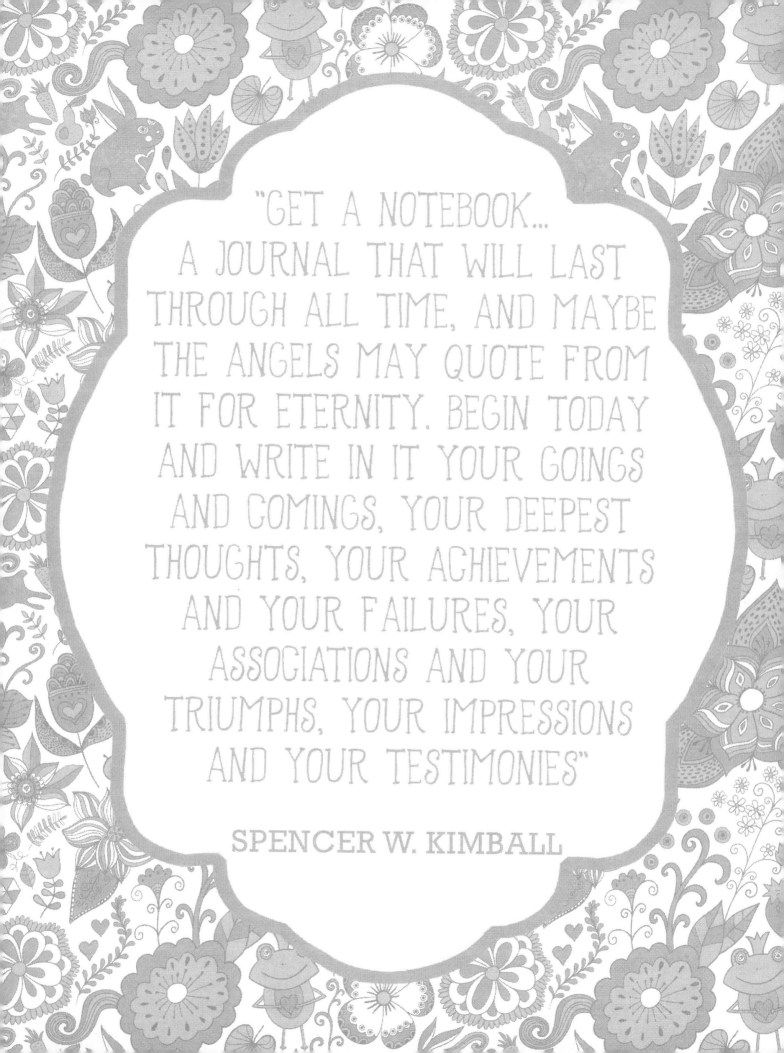

"GET A NOTEBOOK...
A JOURNAL THAT WILL LAST
THROUGH ALL TIME, AND MAYBE
THE ANGELS MAY QUOTE FROM
IT FOR ETERNITY. BEGIN TODAY
AND WRITE IN IT YOUR GOINGS
AND COMINGS, YOUR DEEPEST
THOUGHTS, YOUR ACHIEVEMENTS
AND YOUR FAILURES, YOUR
ASSOCIATIONS AND YOUR
TRIUMPHS, YOUR IMPRESSIONS
AND YOUR TESTIMONIES"

SPENCER W. KIMBALL

"WRITE WHAT SHOULD NOT BE FORGOTTEN."

ISABEL ALLENDE

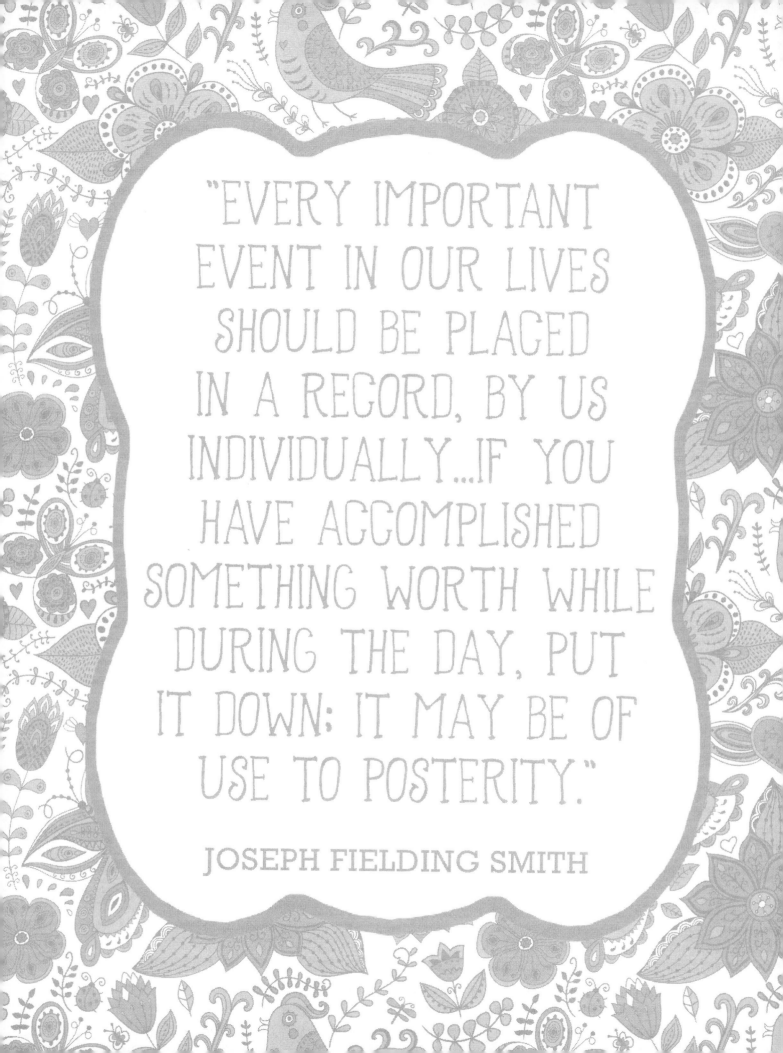

"EVERY IMPORTANT EVENT IN OUR LIVES SHOULD BE PLACED IN A RECORD, BY US INDIVIDUALLY...IF YOU HAVE ACCOMPLISHED SOMETHING WORTH WHILE DURING THE DAY, PUT IT DOWN: IT MAY BE OF USE TO POSTERITY."

JOSEPH FIELDING SMITH

"THE ACT OF WRITING IS THE ACT OF DISCOVERING WHAT YOU BELIEVE."

DAVID HARE

"BY WRITING PERSONAL AND FAMILY HISTORIES, WE ARE HELPED IMMEASURABLY IN GAINING A TRUE, ETERNAL PERSPECTIVE OF LIFE. WRITING OUR HISTORIES WITH THE PROPER BLEND OF FACT AND FEELING (AND SO OFTEN, FEELINGS IN SPIRITUAL THINGS ARE THE REAL FACTS) GIVES US A DEEP SPIRITUAL INSIGHT INTO THE MEANING AND PURPOSE OF OUR LIVES...WRITING OUR HISTORIES WILL CERTAINLY HELP US KEEP OUR EYES ON THE MOST IMPORTANT OF ALL GOALS — EVEN THE GOAL OF ETERNAL LIFE

"THERE IS SOMETHING ETERNAL IN THE VERY NATURE OF WRITING, AS IS SO GRAPHICALLY ILLUSTRATED BY THE SCRIPTURES THEMSELVES. IN A VERY REAL SENSE, OUR PROPERLY WRITTEN HISTORIES ARE A VERY IMPORTANT PART OF OUR FAMILY SCRIPTURE AND BECOME A GREAT SOURCE OF SPIRITUAL STRENGTH TO US AND TO OUR POSTERITY...I HAVE A STRONG FEELING THAT WHEN THIS LIFE IS OVER, OUR PERSONAL AND FAMILY HISTORIES AND THE INFLUENCE THEY WIELD WILL BE OF MUCH GREATER IMPORTANCE THAN WE NOW THINK."

JOHN H. GROBERG

"JOURNAL WRITING IS A VOYAGE TO THE INTERIOR."

CHRISTINA BALDWIN

"THERE IS SOMETHING ABOUT JOURNAL WRITING THAT CAUSES US TO MEDITATE, TO RECOMMIT, AND TO RECEIVE SPIRITUAL IMPRESSIONS IN THE PROCESS OF SUCH PONDERING. FREQUENTLY, YOU WILL HAVE CAUSE TO REJOICE AT HOW THE LORD HAS BEEN SENSITIVELY INVOLVED IN GUIDING AND WATCHING OVER YOU AND THOSE YOU LOVE AND CARE ABOUT."

L. EDWARD BROWN

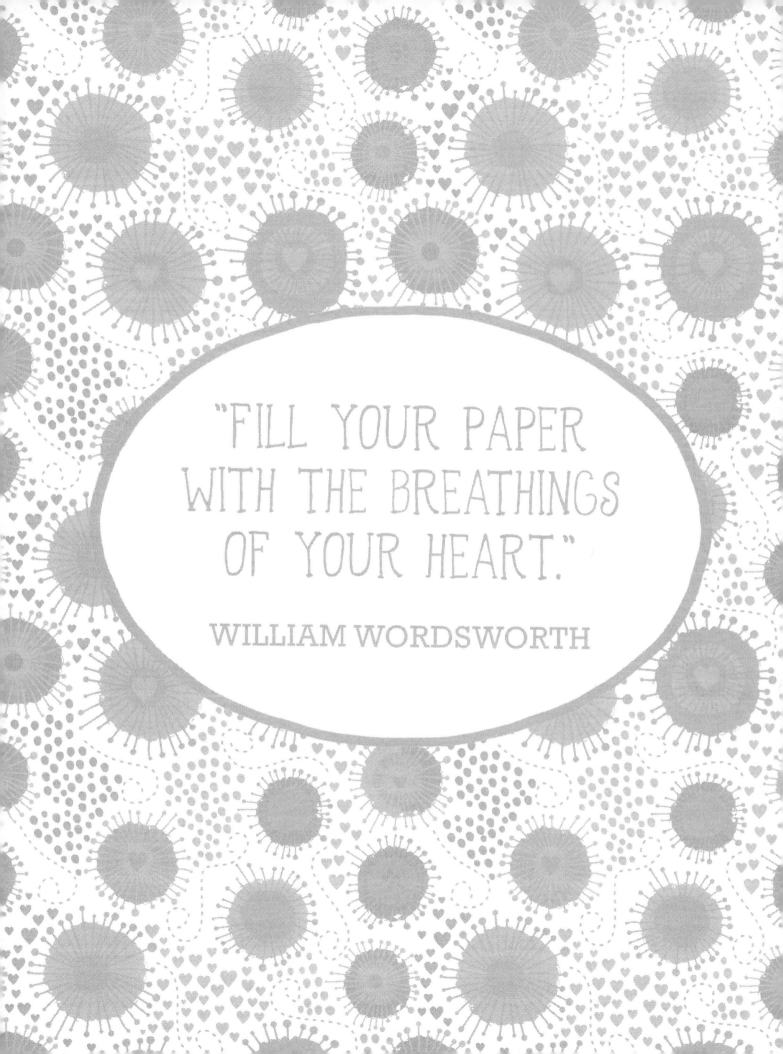

"FILL YOUR PAPER
WITH THE BREATHINGS
OF YOUR HEART."

WILLIAM WORDSWORTH

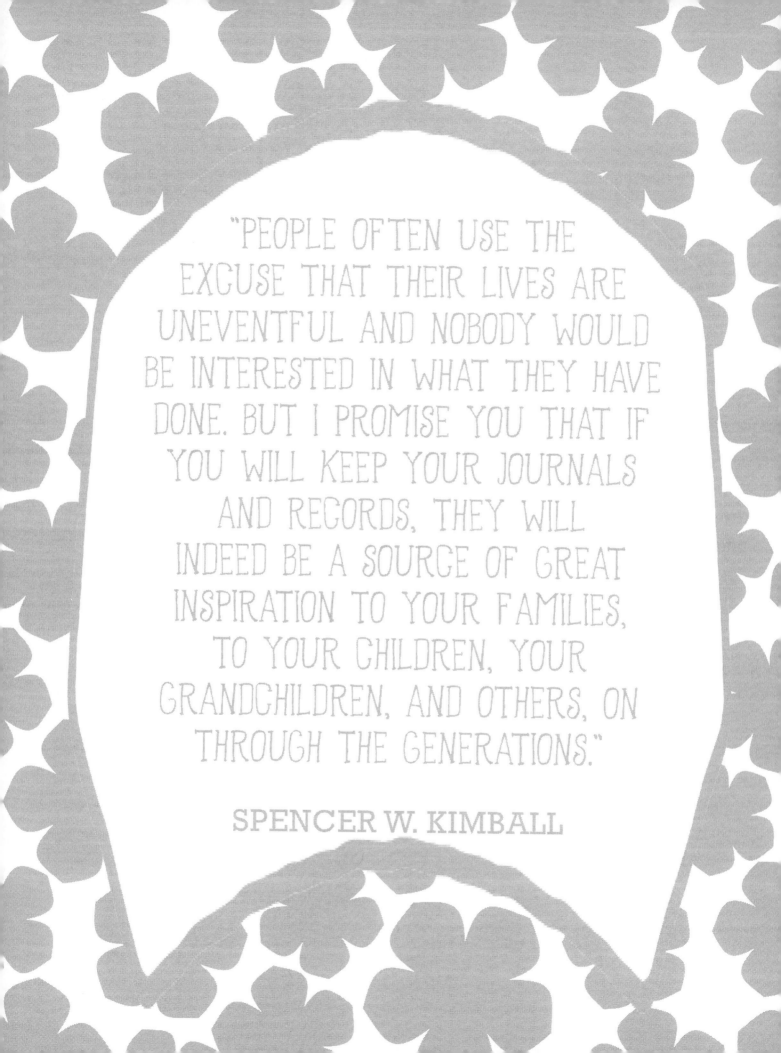

"PEOPLE OFTEN USE THE EXCUSE THAT THEIR LIVES ARE UNEVENTFUL AND NOBODY WOULD BE INTERESTED IN WHAT THEY HAVE DONE. BUT I PROMISE YOU THAT IF YOU WILL KEEP YOUR JOURNALS AND RECORDS, THEY WILL INDEED BE A SOURCE OF GREAT INSPIRATION TO YOUR FAMILIES, TO YOUR CHILDREN, YOUR GRANDCHILDREN, AND OTHERS, ON THROUGH THE GENERATIONS."

SPENCER W. KIMBALL

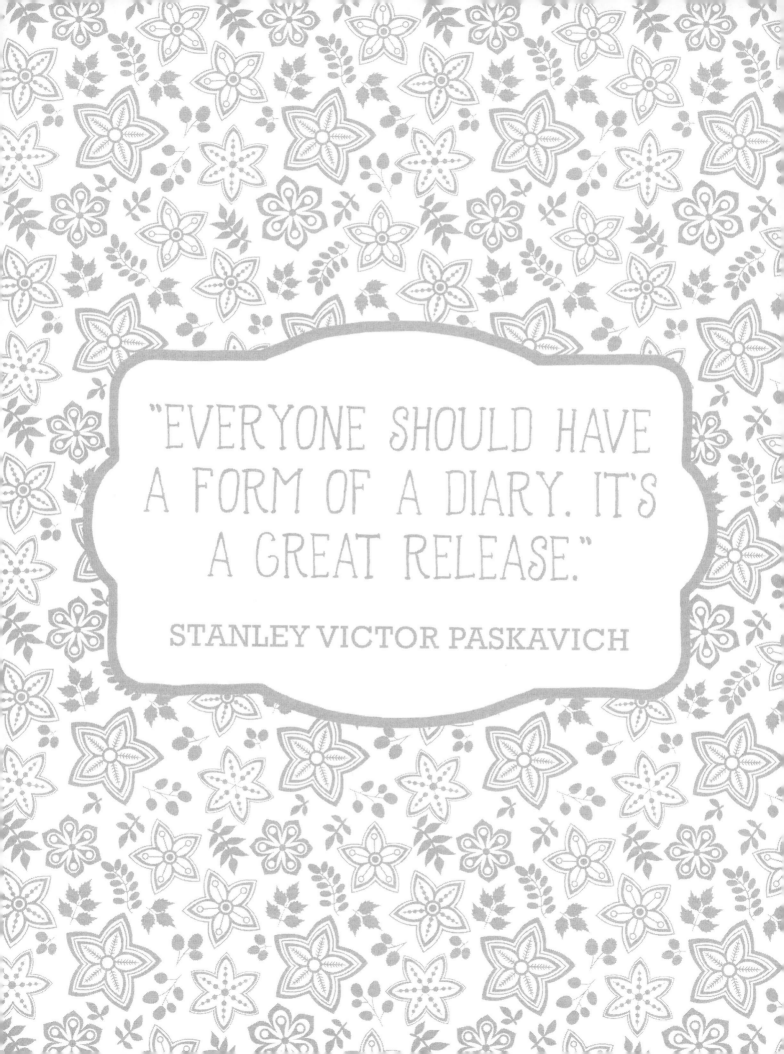

"EVERYONE SHOULD HAVE A FORM OF A DIARY. IT'S A GREAT RELEASE."

STANLEY VICTOR PASKAVICH

"WHILE WALKING IN A RAPID STREAM WE CANNOT TREAD TWICE IN THE SAME WATER. NEITHER CAN WE SPEND TWICE THE SAME TIME. WHEN WE PASS OUT OF THAT DOOR, THE WORK OF THIS MEETING WILL BE CLOSED TO US FOREVER. WE SHALL NEVER SPEND THE TIME OF THIS EVENING AGAIN. THEN SHOULD WE NOT KEEP A RECORD OF OUR WORK, TEACHINGS, AND COUNSEL."

WILFORD WOODRUFF

"WHAT HAPPENS TO US IS NOT AS IMPORTANT AS THE MEANING WE ASSIGN TO IT. JOURNALING HELPS SORT THIS OUT."

MICHAEL HYATT

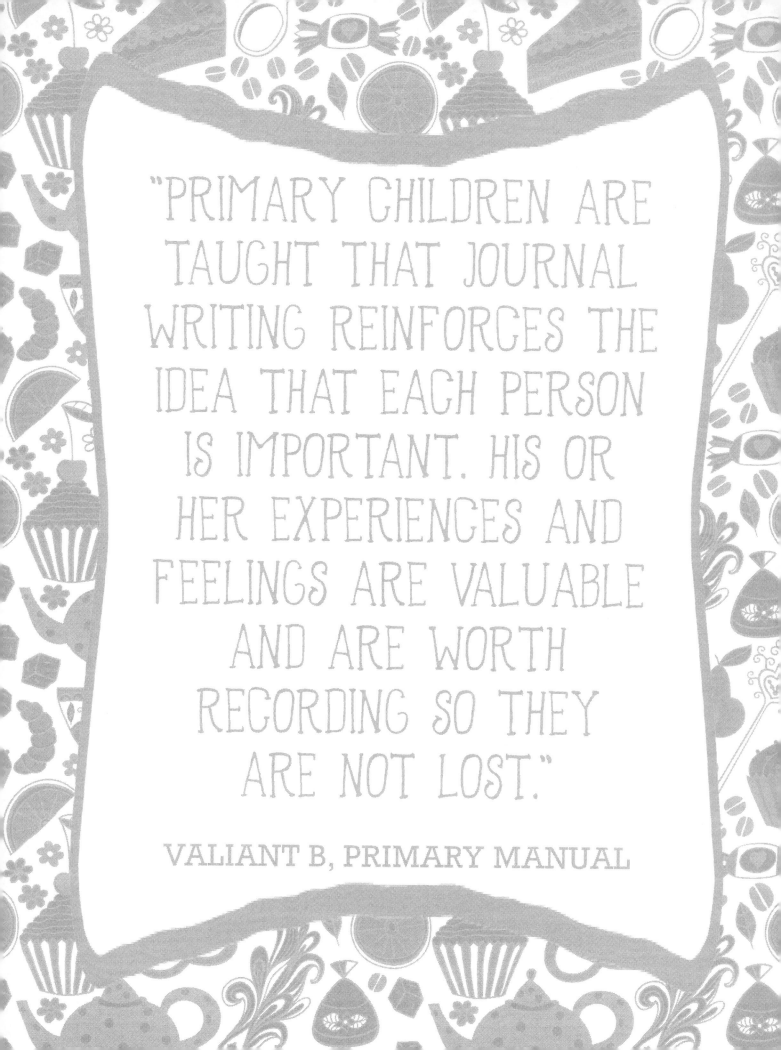

"PRIMARY CHILDREN ARE TAUGHT THAT JOURNAL WRITING REINFORCES THE IDEA THAT EACH PERSON IS IMPORTANT. HIS OR HER EXPERIENCES AND FEELINGS ARE VALUABLE AND ARE WORTH RECORDING SO THEY ARE NOT LOST."

VALIANT B, PRIMARY MANUAL

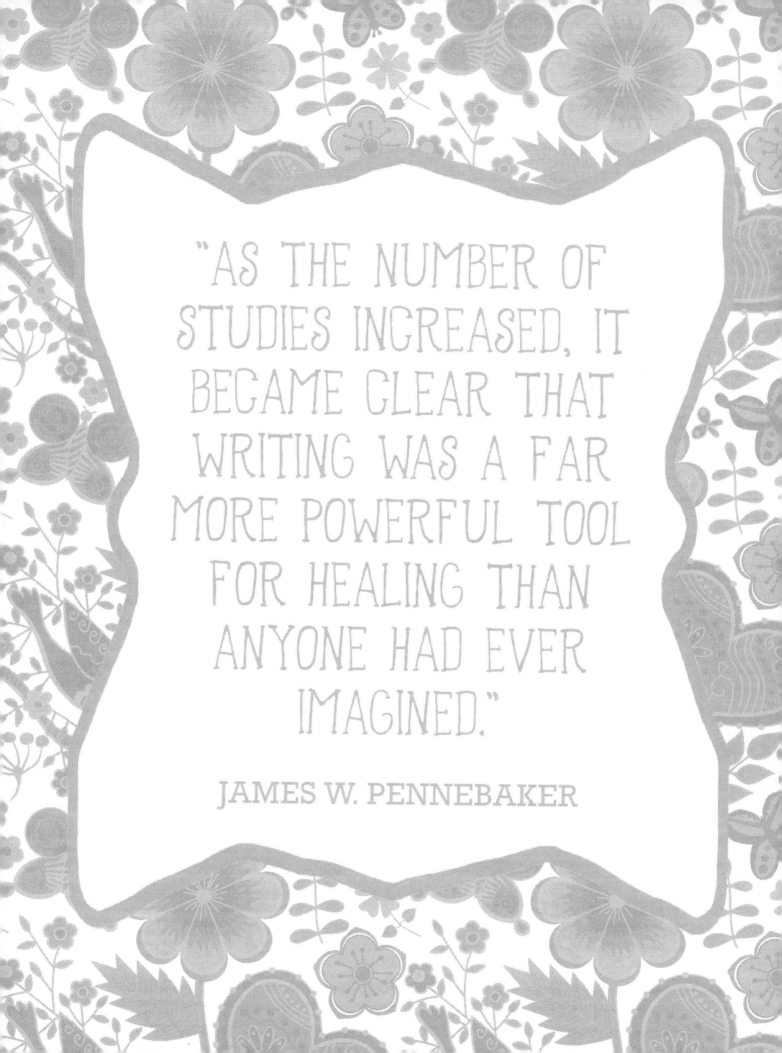

"AS THE NUMBER OF STUDIES INCREASED, IT BECAME CLEAR THAT WRITING WAS A FAR MORE POWERFUL TOOL FOR HEALING THAN ANYONE HAD EVER IMAGINED."

JAMES W. PENNEBAKER

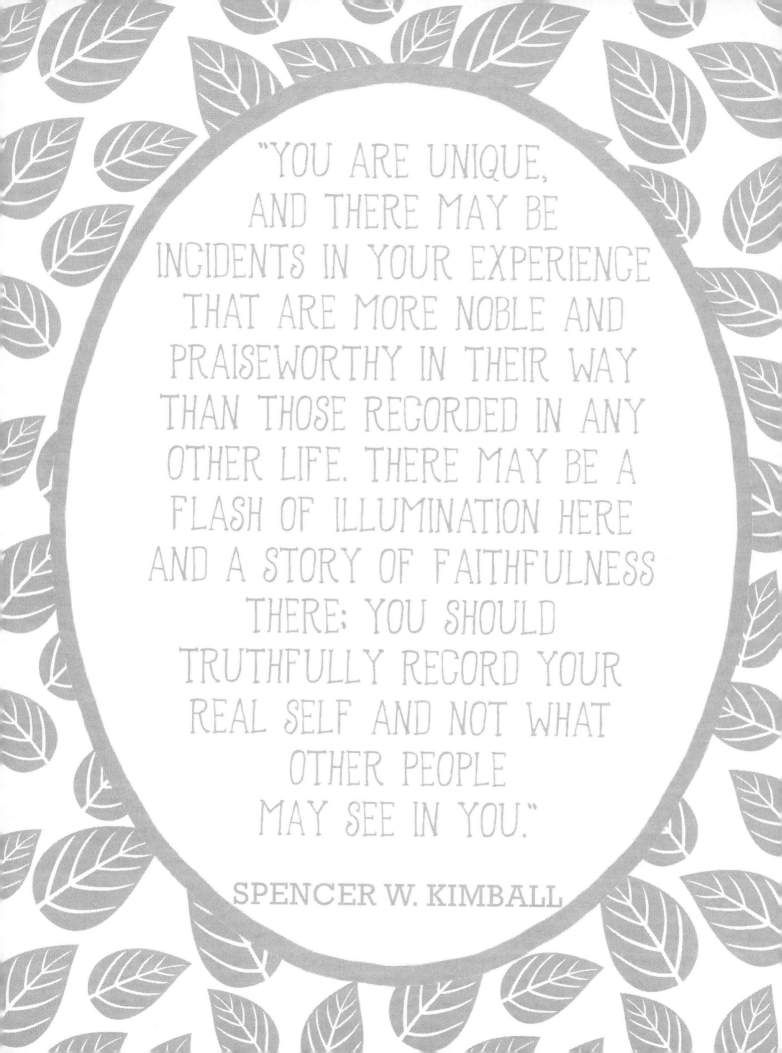

"YOU ARE UNIQUE, AND THERE MAY BE INCIDENTS IN YOUR EXPERIENCE THAT ARE MORE NOBLE AND PRAISEWORTHY IN THEIR WAY THAN THOSE RECORDED IN ANY OTHER LIFE. THERE MAY BE A FLASH OF ILLUMINATION HERE AND A STORY OF FAITHFULNESS THERE; YOU SHOULD TRUTHFULLY RECORD YOUR REAL SELF AND NOT WHAT OTHER PEOPLE MAY SEE IN YOU."

SPENCER W. KIMBALL

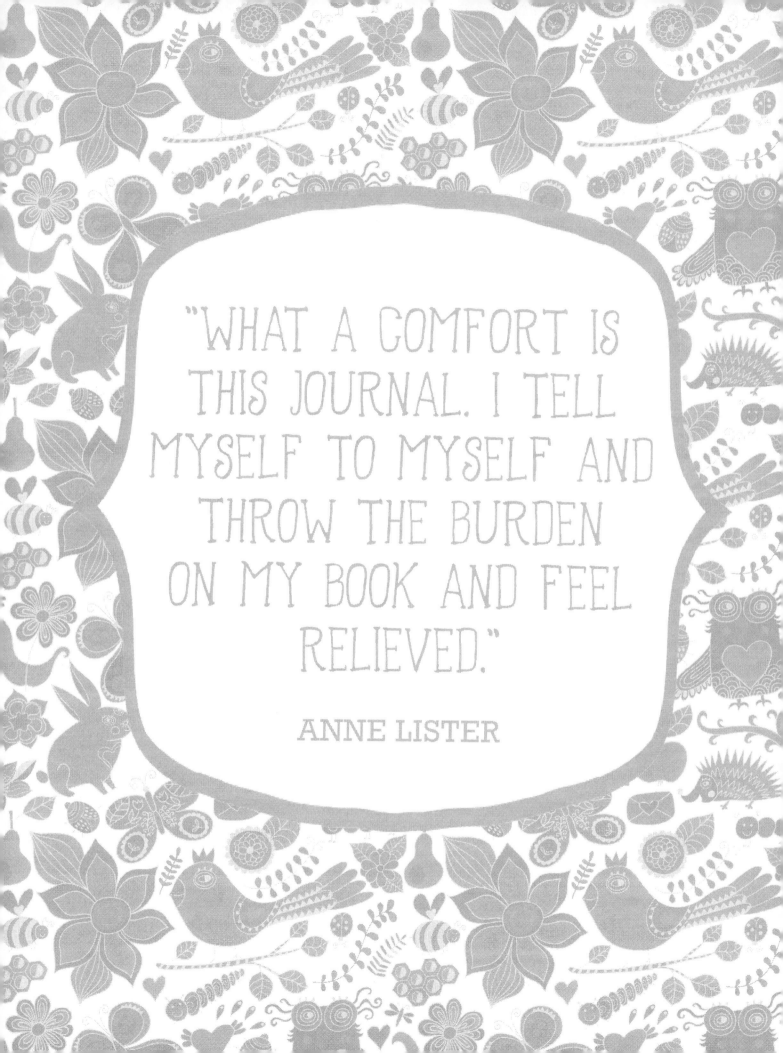

"WHAT A COMFORT IS THIS JOURNAL. I TELL MYSELF TO MYSELF AND THROW THE BURDEN ON MY BOOK AND FEEL RELIEVED."

ANNE LISTER

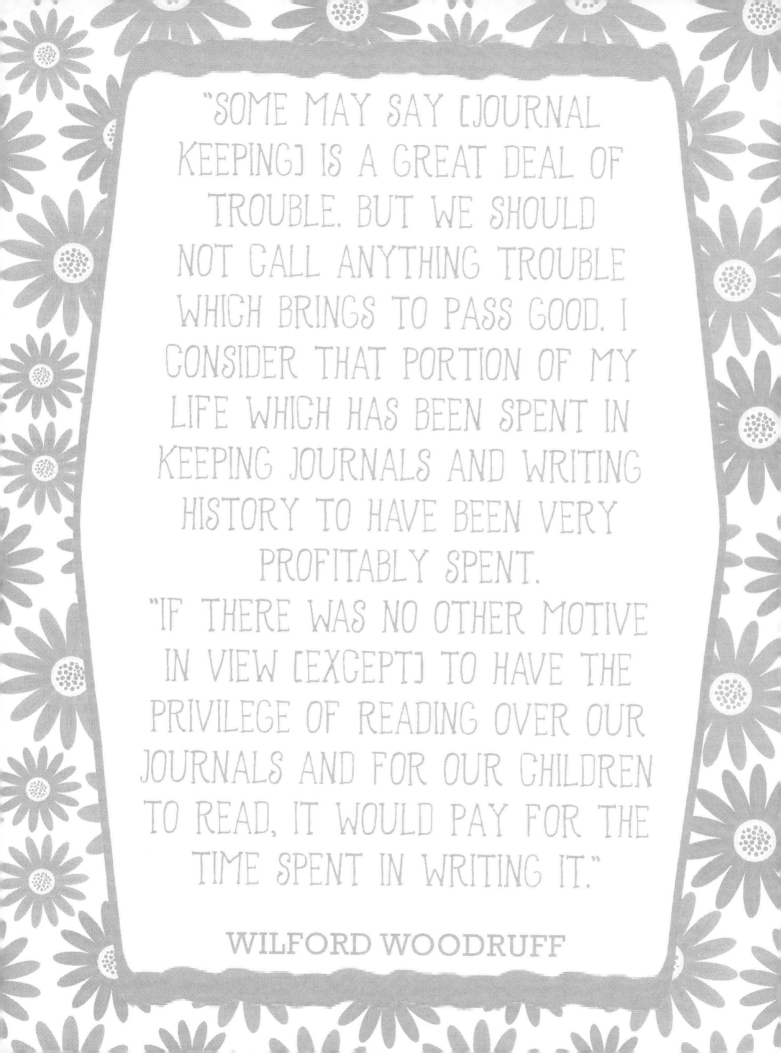

"SOME MAY SAY [JOURNAL KEEPING] IS A GREAT DEAL OF TROUBLE. BUT WE SHOULD NOT CALL ANYTHING TROUBLE WHICH BRINGS TO PASS GOOD. I CONSIDER THAT PORTION OF MY LIFE WHICH HAS BEEN SPENT IN KEEPING JOURNALS AND WRITING HISTORY TO HAVE BEEN VERY PROFITABLY SPENT.

"IF THERE WAS NO OTHER MOTIVE IN VIEW [EXCEPT] TO HAVE THE PRIVILEGE OF READING OVER OUR JOURNALS AND FOR OUR CHILDREN TO READ, IT WOULD PAY FOR THE TIME SPENT IN WRITING IT."

WILFORD WOODRUFF

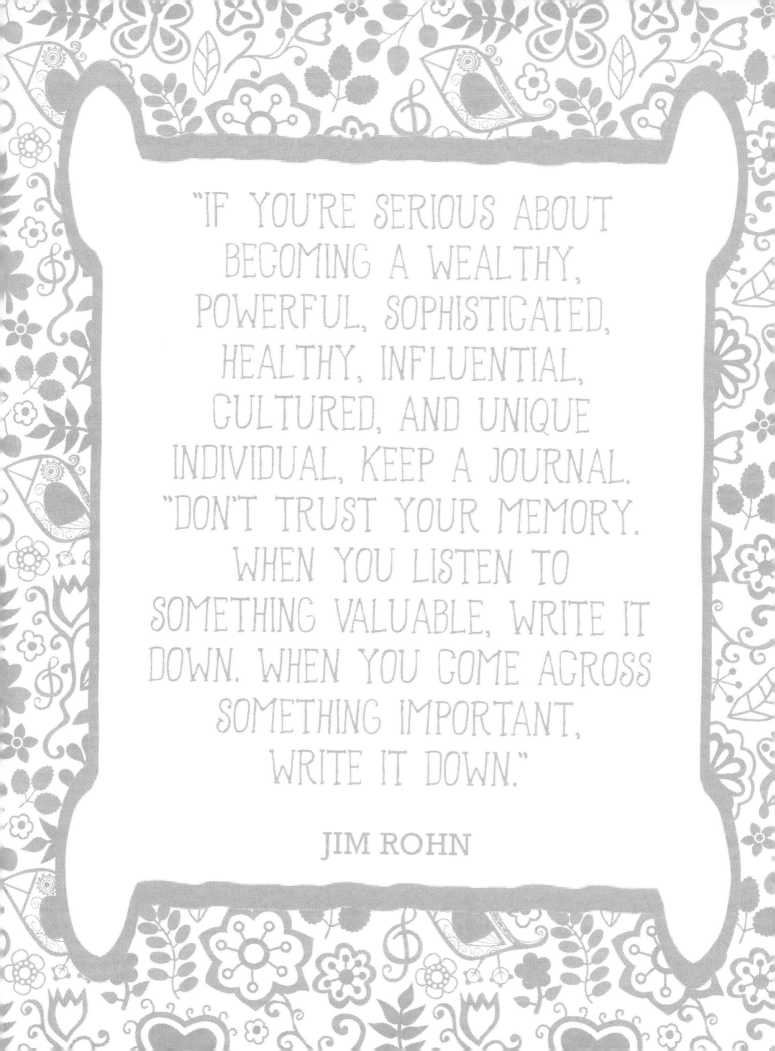

"IF YOU'RE SERIOUS ABOUT
BECOMING A WEALTHY,
POWERFUL, SOPHISTICATED,
HEALTHY, INFLUENTIAL,
CULTURED, AND UNIQUE
INDIVIDUAL, KEEP A JOURNAL.
"DON'T TRUST YOUR MEMORY.
WHEN YOU LISTEN TO
SOMETHING VALUABLE, WRITE IT
DOWN. WHEN YOU COME ACROSS
SOMETHING IMPORTANT,
WRITE IT DOWN."

JIM ROHN

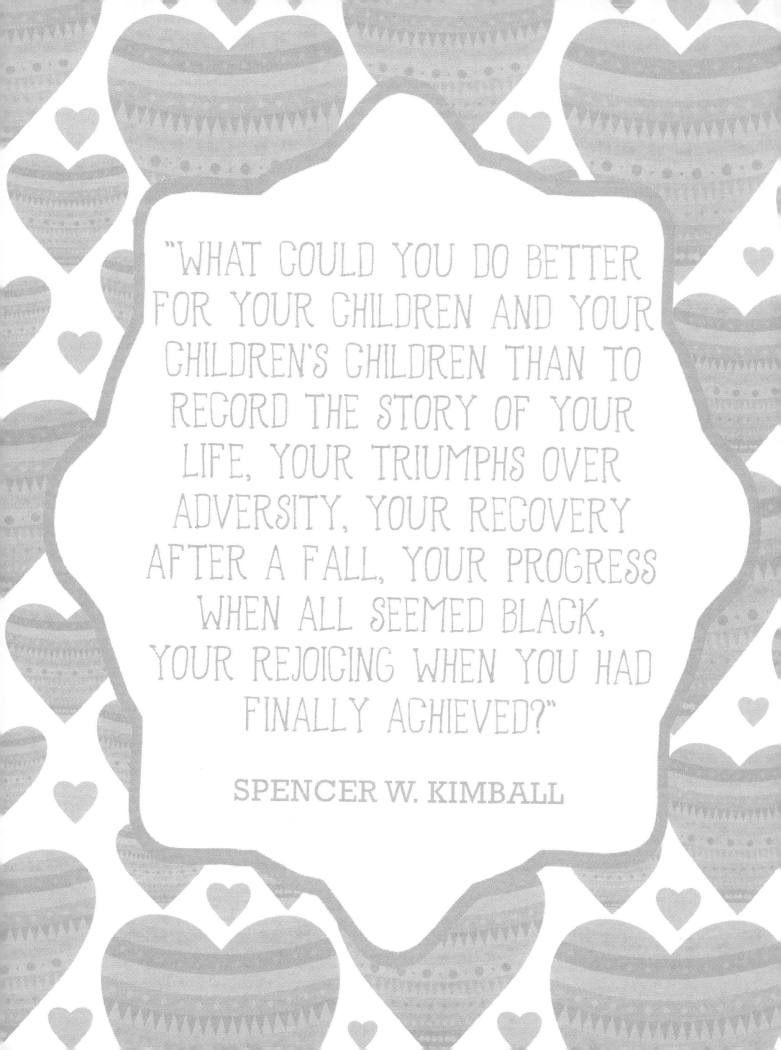

"WHAT COULD YOU DO BETTER FOR YOUR CHILDREN AND YOUR CHILDREN'S CHILDREN THAN TO RECORD THE STORY OF YOUR LIFE, YOUR TRIUMPHS OVER ADVERSITY, YOUR RECOVERY AFTER A FALL, YOUR PROGRESS WHEN ALL SEEMED BLACK, YOUR REJOICING WHEN YOU HAD FINALLY ACHIEVED?"

SPENCER W. KIMBALL

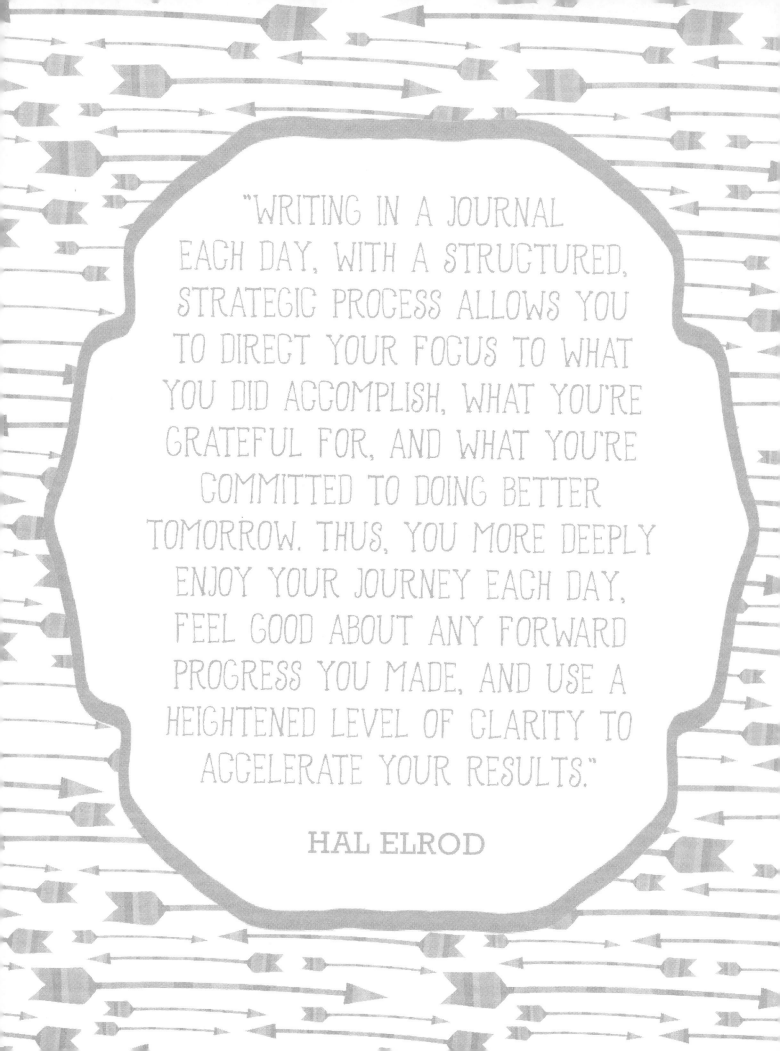

"WRITING IN A JOURNAL EACH DAY, WITH A STRUCTURED, STRATEGIC PROCESS ALLOWS YOU TO DIRECT YOUR FOCUS TO WHAT YOU DID ACCOMPLISH, WHAT YOU'RE GRATEFUL FOR, AND WHAT YOU'RE COMMITTED TO DOING BETTER TOMORROW. THUS, YOU MORE DEEPLY ENJOY YOUR JOURNEY EACH DAY, FEEL GOOD ABOUT ANY FORWARD PROGRESS YOU MADE, AND USE A HEIGHTENED LEVEL OF CLARITY TO ACCELERATE YOUR RESULTS."

HAL ELROD

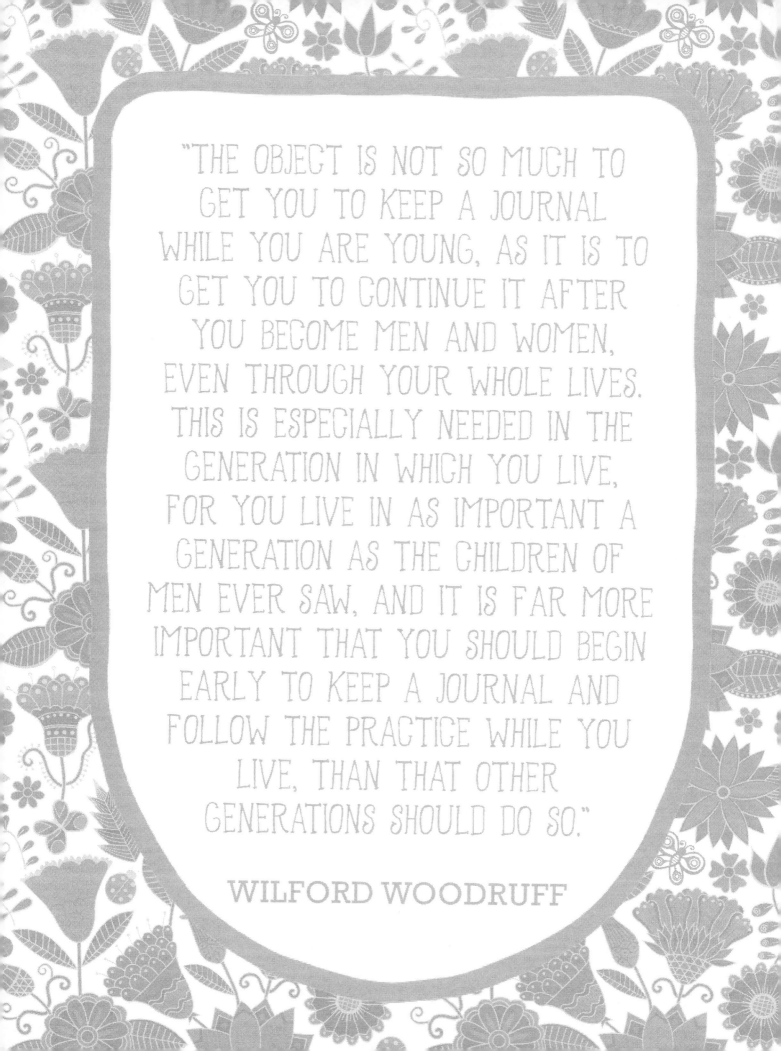

"THE OBJECT IS NOT SO MUCH TO GET YOU TO KEEP A JOURNAL WHILE YOU ARE YOUNG, AS IT IS TO GET YOU TO CONTINUE IT AFTER YOU BECOME MEN AND WOMEN, EVEN THROUGH YOUR WHOLE LIVES. THIS IS ESPECIALLY NEEDED IN THE GENERATION IN WHICH YOU LIVE, FOR YOU LIVE IN AS IMPORTANT A GENERATION AS THE CHILDREN OF MEN EVER SAW, AND IT IS FAR MORE IMPORTANT THAT YOU SHOULD BEGIN EARLY TO KEEP A JOURNAL AND FOLLOW THE PRACTICE WHILE YOU LIVE, THAN THAT OTHER GENERATIONS SHOULD DO SO."

WILFORD WOODRUFF

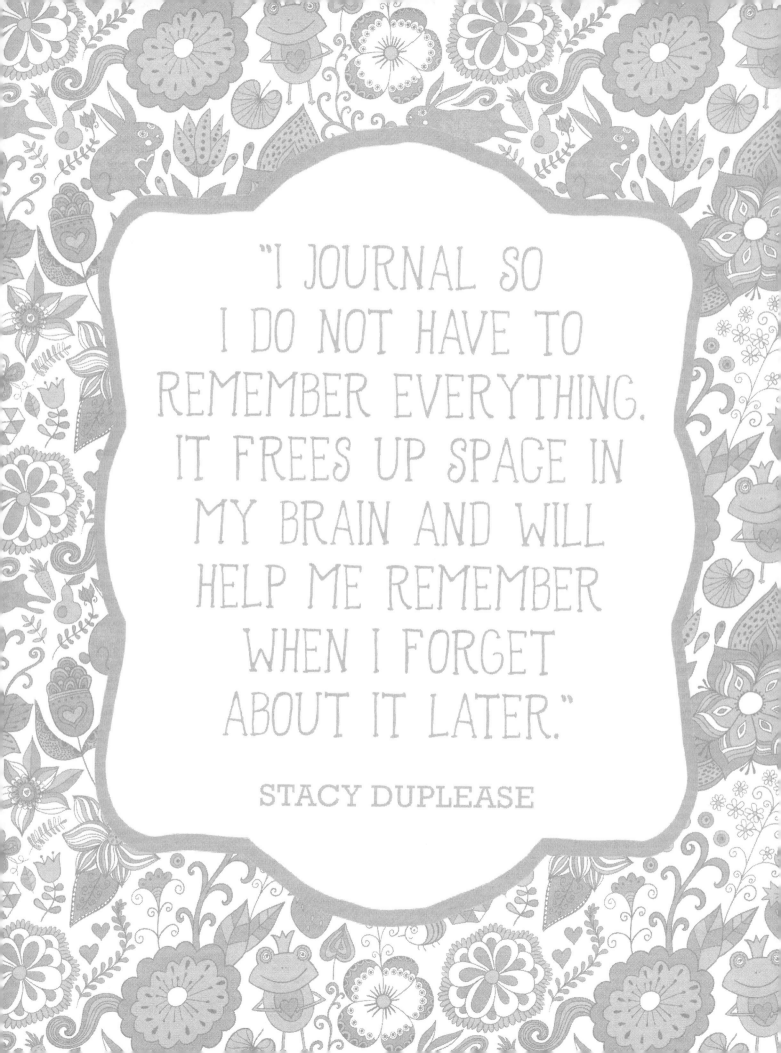

"I JOURNAL SO
I DO NOT HAVE TO
REMEMBER EVERYTHING.
IT FREES UP SPACE IN
MY BRAIN AND WILL
HELP ME REMEMBER
WHEN I FORGET
ABOUT IT LATER."

STACY DUPLEASE

"I PROMISE YOU
THAT IF YOU WILL
KEEP YOUR JOURNALS AND
RECORDS, THEY WILL INDEED BE A
SOURCE OF GREAT INSPIRATION TO
YOUR FAMILIES, TO YOUR CHILDREN,
YOUR GRANDCHILDREN, AND OTHERS, ON
THROUGH THE GENERATIONS. EACH OF US
IS IMPORTANT TO THOSE WHO ARE NEAR
AND DEAR TO US AND AS OUR POSTERITY
READ OF OUR LIFE'S EXPERIENCES,
THEY, TOO, WILL COME TO KNOW AND
LOVE US. AND IN THAT GLORIOUS DAY
WHEN OUR FAMILIES ARE TOGETHER IN
THE ETERNITIES, WE WILL ALREADY BE
ACQUAINTED."

SPENCER W. KIMBALL

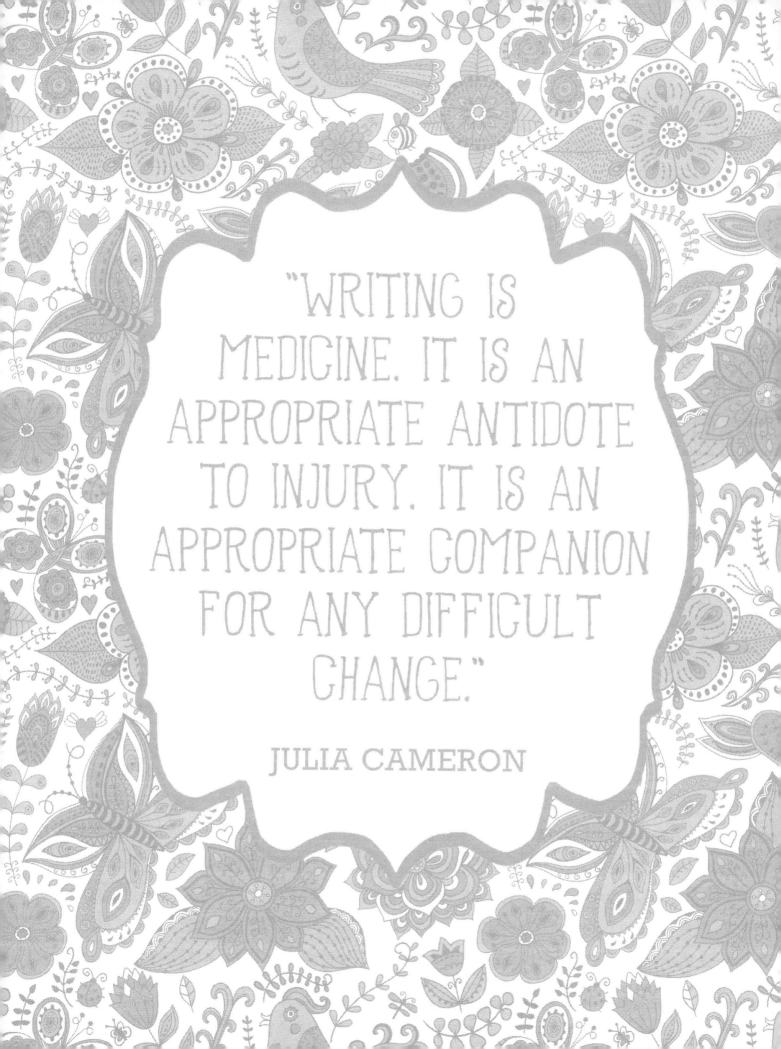

"WRITING IS MEDICINE. IT IS AN APPROPRIATE ANTIDOTE TO INJURY. IT IS AN APPROPRIATE COMPANION FOR ANY DIFFICULT CHANGE."

JULIA CAMERON

"YOU [NEED] TO KEEP A JOURNAL. FIRST OF ALL, YOUR LIFE REALLY IS INTERESTING. YOU ARE UNIQUE, AND YOUR EXPERIENCES ARE DIFFERENT FROM ANYONE ELSE'S. YOU DON'T HAVE TO SEE MIRACLES OR CHANGE THE WORLD TO HAVE SOMETHING WORTHY TO RECORD IN YOUR JOURNAL—YOUR THOUGHTS AND FEELINGS ARE EXCITING ENOUGH."

QUESTIONS AND ANSWERS, NEW ERA, SEPT. 2003

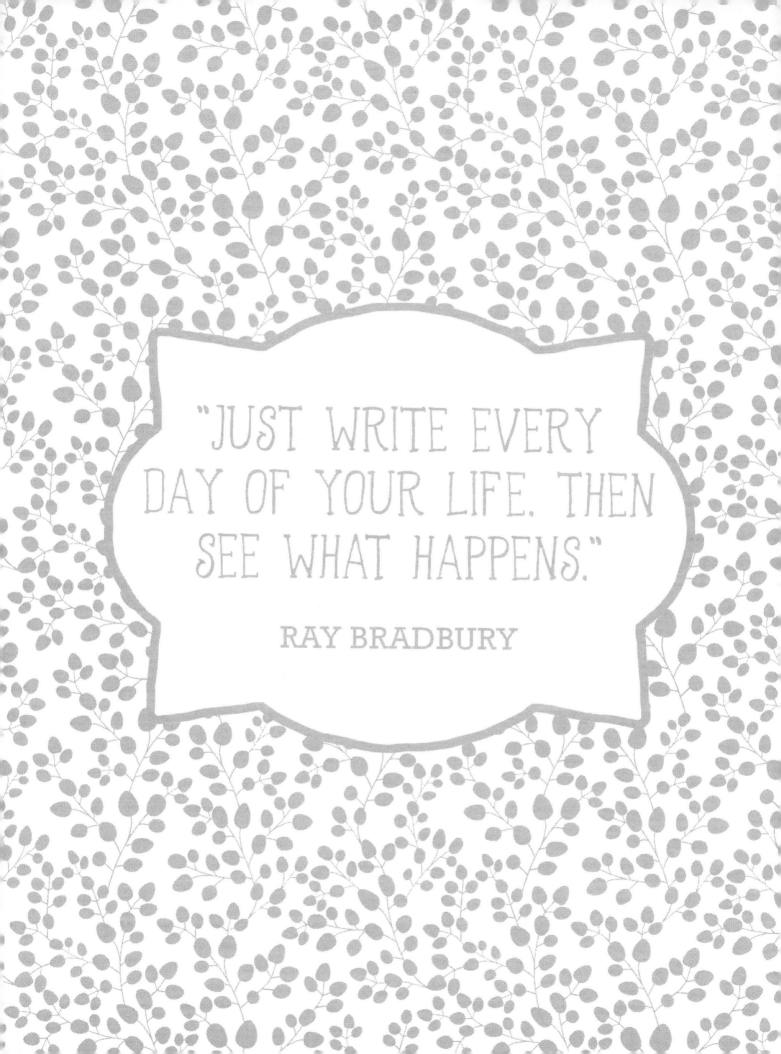

"JUST WRITE EVERY DAY OF YOUR LIFE. THEN SEE WHAT HAPPENS."

RAY BRADBURY

"ANOTHER REASON TO KEEP A JOURNAL IS FOR YOUR POSTERITY. BUT IT'S NOT THE MOST IMPORTANT ONE. THE BIGGEST REASON TO WRITE IN YOUR JOURNAL IS FOR YOU. EVEN IF NO ONE ELSE EVER LAYS EYES ON YOUR JOURNALS, IT DOESN'T MATTER."

QUESTIONS AND ANSWERS, NEW ERA, SEPT. 2003

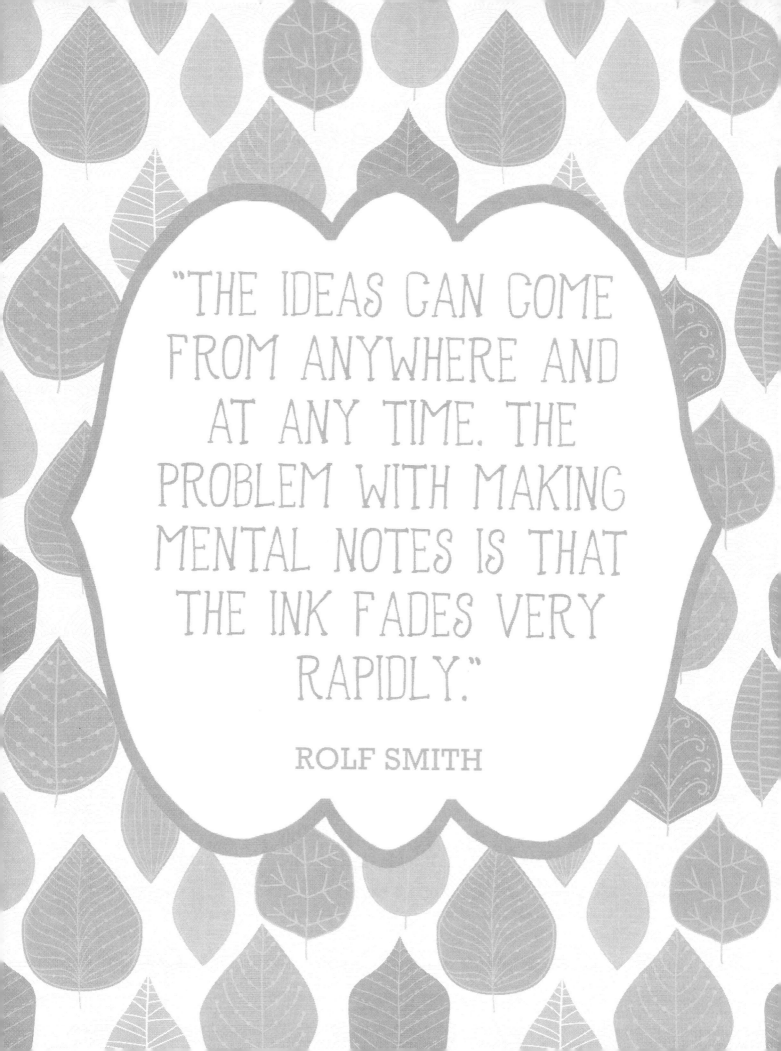

"THE IDEAS CAN COME FROM ANYWHERE AND AT ANY TIME. THE PROBLEM WITH MAKING MENTAL NOTES IS THAT THE INK FADES VERY RAPIDLY."

ROLF SMITH

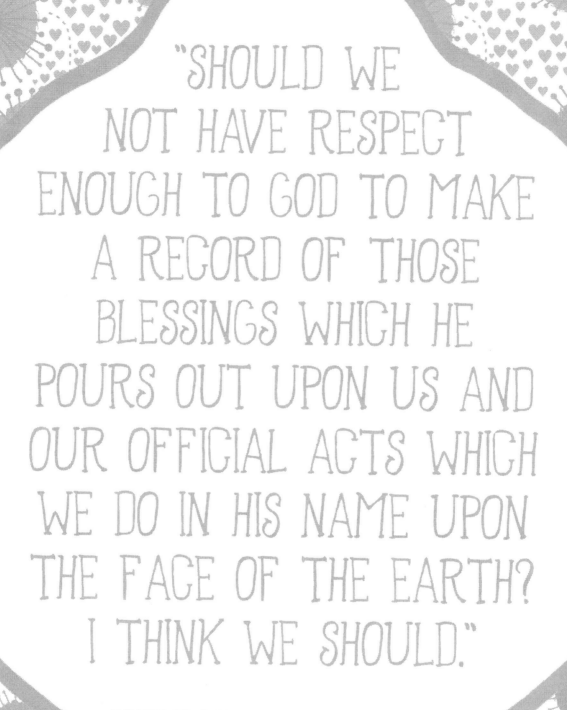

"SHOULD WE NOT HAVE RESPECT ENOUGH TO GOD TO MAKE A RECORD OF THOSE BLESSINGS WHICH HE POURS OUT UPON US AND OUR OFFICIAL ACTS WHICH WE DO IN HIS NAME UPON THE FACE OF THE EARTH? I THINK WE SHOULD."

WILFORD WOODRUFF

"JOURNALING IS LIKE WHISPERING TO ONE'S SELF AND LISTENING AT THE SAME TIME."

MINA MURRAY, DRACULA

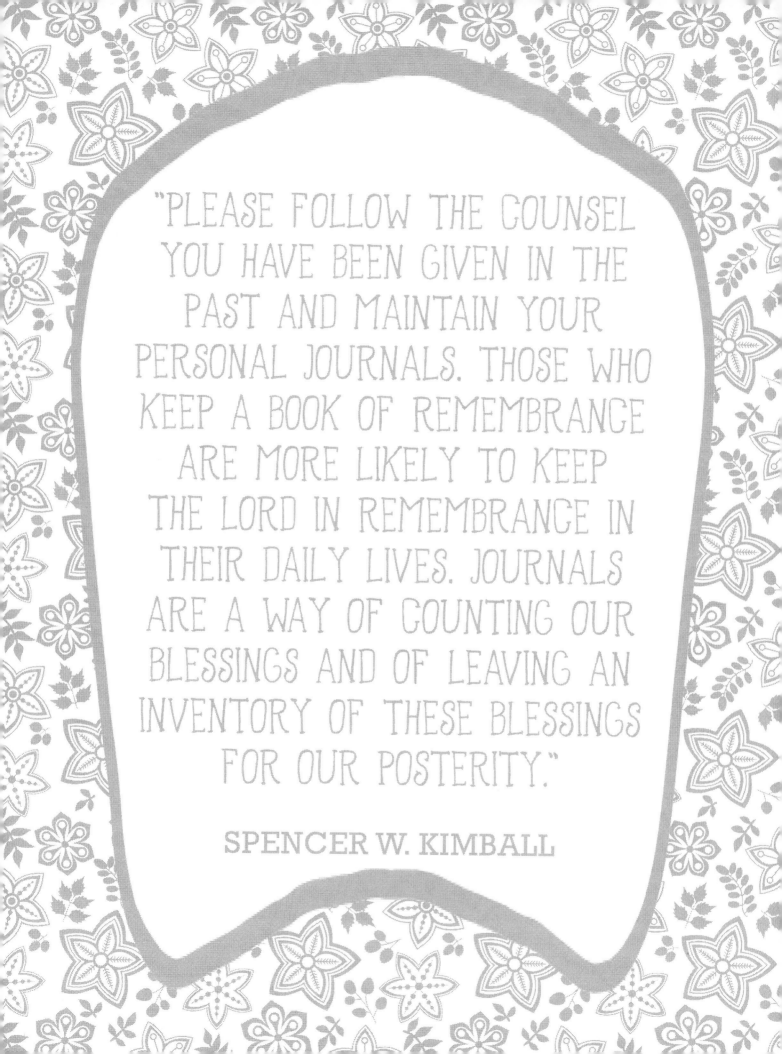

"PLEASE FOLLOW THE COUNSEL
YOU HAVE BEEN GIVEN IN THE
PAST AND MAINTAIN YOUR
PERSONAL JOURNALS. THOSE WHO
KEEP A BOOK OF REMEMBRANCE
ARE MORE LIKELY TO KEEP
THE LORD IN REMEMBRANCE IN
THEIR DAILY LIVES. JOURNALS
ARE A WAY OF COUNTING OUR
BLESSINGS AND OF LEAVING AN
INVENTORY OF THESE BLESSINGS
FOR OUR POSTERITY."

SPENCER W. KIMBALL

"WHATEVER IT IS THAT YOU WRITE, PUTTING WORDS ON THE PAGE IS A FORM OF THERAPY THAT DOESN'T COST A DIME."

DIANA RAAB

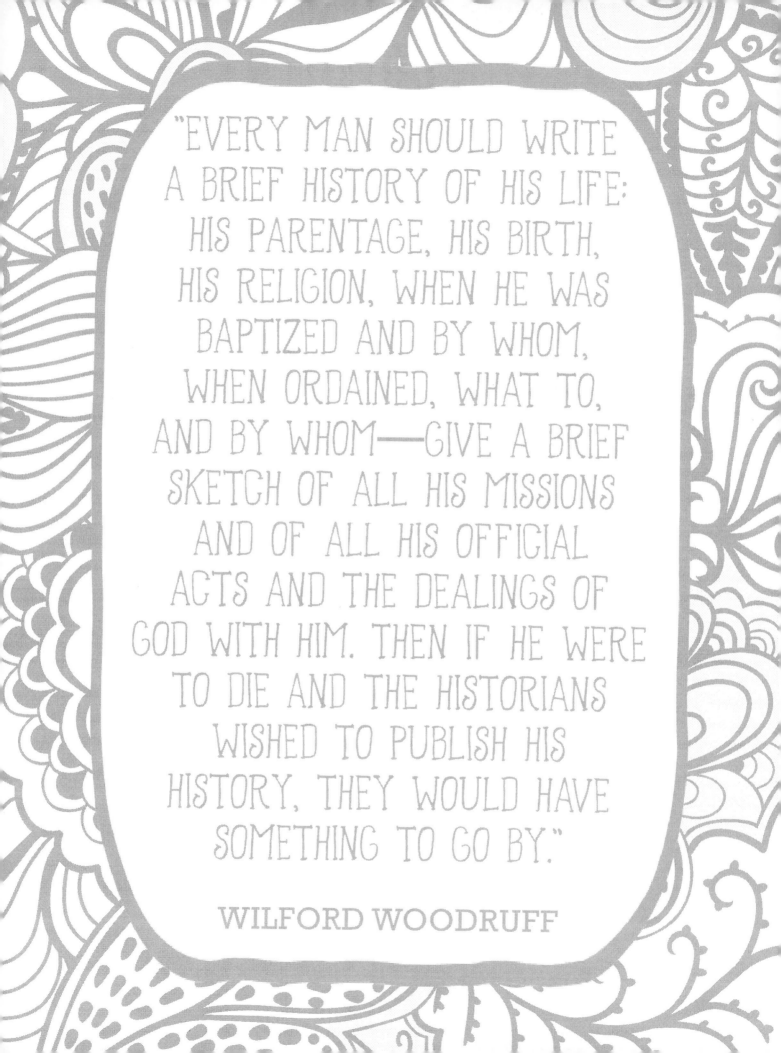

"EVERY MAN SHOULD WRITE
A BRIEF HISTORY OF HIS LIFE:
HIS PARENTAGE, HIS BIRTH,
HIS RELIGION, WHEN HE WAS
BAPTIZED AND BY WHOM,
WHEN ORDAINED, WHAT TO,
AND BY WHOM—GIVE A BRIEF
SKETCH OF ALL HIS MISSIONS
AND OF ALL HIS OFFICIAL
ACTS AND THE DEALINGS OF
GOD WITH HIM. THEN IF HE WERE
TO DIE AND THE HISTORIANS
WISHED TO PUBLISH HIS
HISTORY, THEY WOULD HAVE
SOMETHING TO GO BY."

WILFORD WOODRUFF

"THERE ARE A THOUSAND THOUGHTS LYING WITHIN A MAN THAT HE DOES NOT KNOW TILL HE TAKES UP THE PEN TO WRITE."

WILLIAM MAKEPEACE THACKERAY

"I WOULD ADVISE YOU TO GET ALL OF YOUR BLESSINGS WRITTEN AND PRESERVE THEM...I DO FEEL TO ENJOIN IT UPON YOU TO MAKE A RECORD OF EVERY OFFICIAL ACT OF YOUR LIFE. IF YOU BAPTIZE, CONFIRM, ORDAIN, OR BLESS ANY PERSON OR ADMINISTER TO THE SICK, WRITE AN ACCOUNT OF IT. IF EVERY MAN WILL DO THIS, THE CHURCH CAN WRITE A CORRECT ACCOUNT OF IT...IF THE POWER AND BLESSINGS OF GOD ARE MADE MANIFEST IN YOUR PRESERVATION FROM DANGER...YOU SHOULD MAKE A RECORD OF IT. KEEP AN ACCOUNT OF THE DEALINGS OF GOD WITH YOU DAILY. I HAVE WRITTEN ALL THE BLESSINGS I HAVE RECEIVED, AND I WOULD NOT TAKE GOLD FOR THEM."

WILFORD WOODRUFF

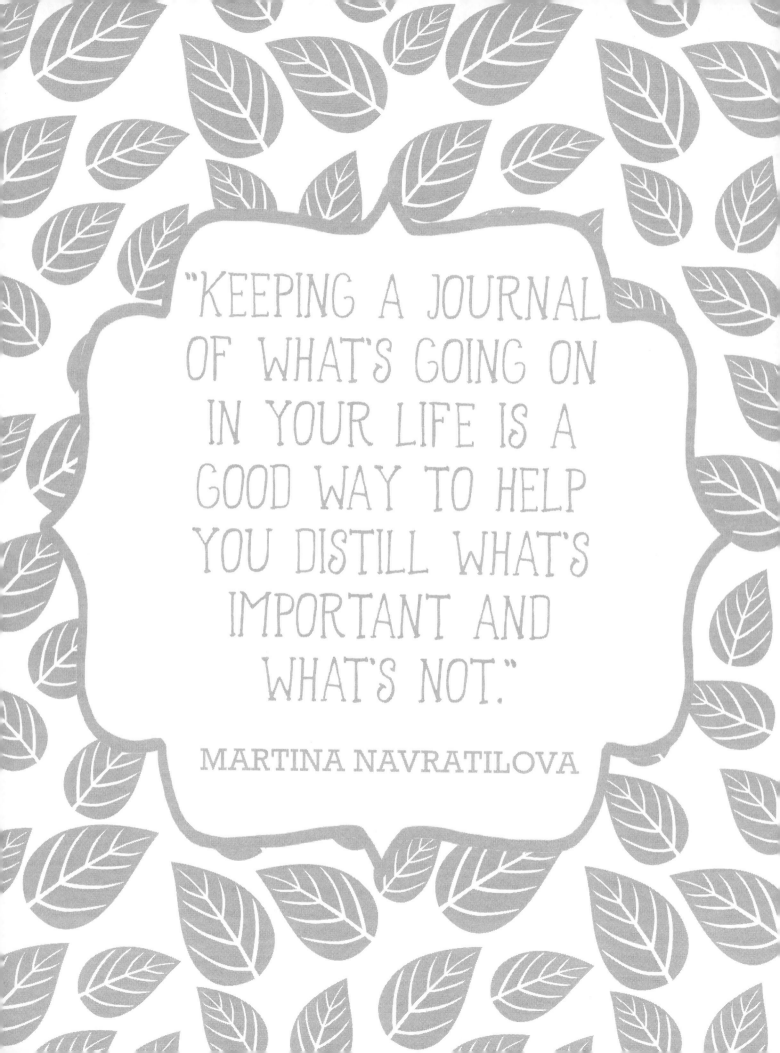

"KEEPING A JOURNAL OF WHAT'S GOING ON IN YOUR LIFE IS A GOOD WAY TO HELP YOU DISTILL WHAT'S IMPORTANT AND WHAT'S NOT."

MARTINA NAVRATILOVA

"IN MY LIFE, I HAD TO DISCOVER THAT WRITING IN MY JOURNAL IS VALUABLE FOR ME—WHETHER MY GRANDCHILDREN EVER READ IT OR NOT."

BRAD WILCOX

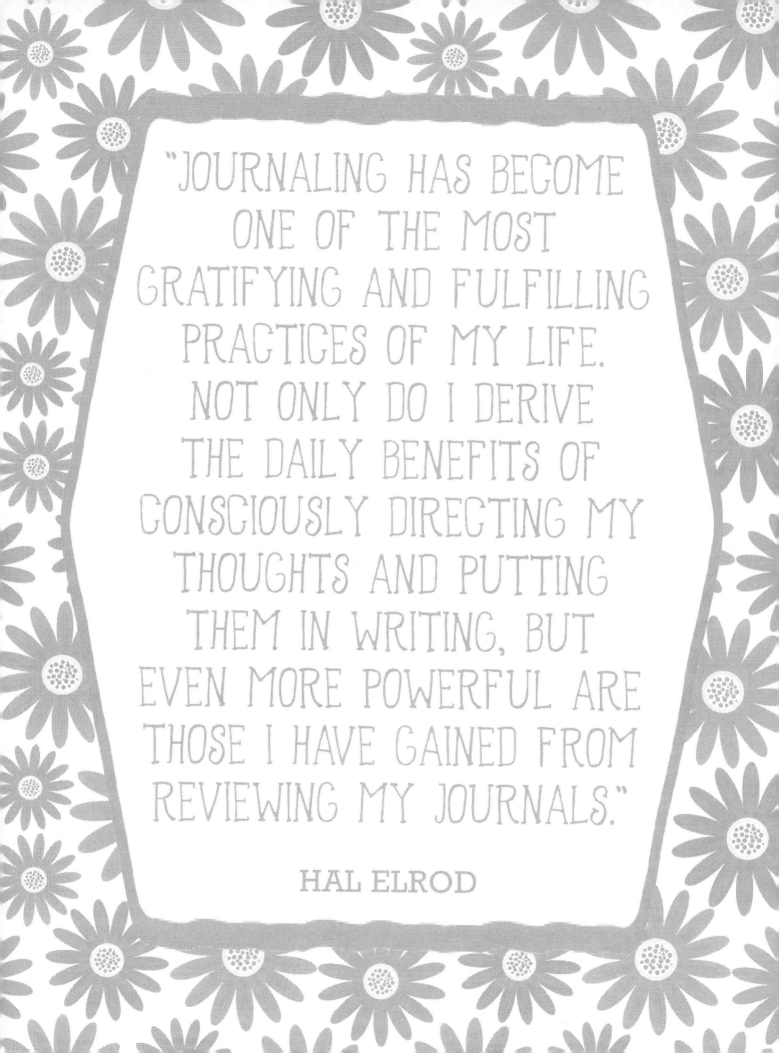

"JOURNALING HAS BECOME ONE OF THE MOST GRATIFYING AND FULFILLING PRACTICES OF MY LIFE. NOT ONLY DO I DERIVE THE DAILY BENEFITS OF CONSCIOUSLY DIRECTING MY THOUGHTS AND PUTTING THEM IN WRITING, BUT EVEN MORE POWERFUL ARE THOSE I HAVE GAINED FROM REVIEWING MY JOURNALS."

HAL ELROD

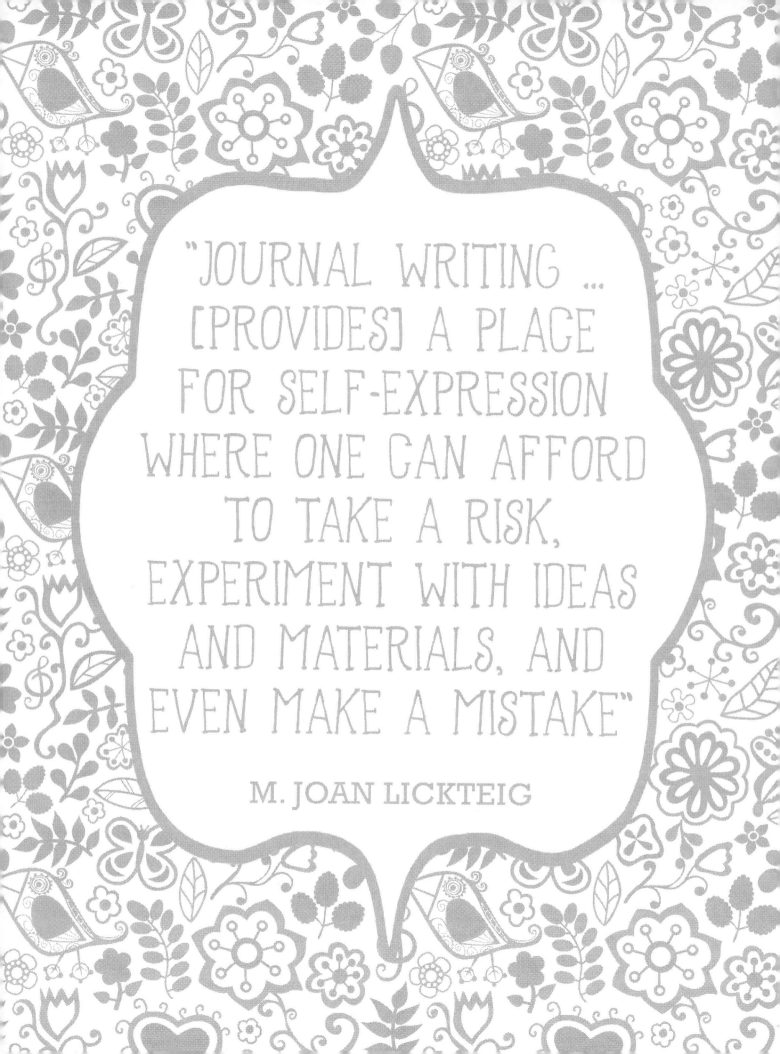

"JOURNAL WRITING ... [PROVIDES] A PLACE FOR SELF-EXPRESSION WHERE ONE CAN AFFORD TO TAKE A RISK, EXPERIMENT WITH IDEAS AND MATERIALS, AND EVEN MAKE A MISTAKE"

M. JOAN LICKTEIG

"THOUGHTS ARE CREATED IN THE ACT OF WRITING. [IT IS A MYTH THAT] YOU MUST HAVE SOMETHING TO SAY IN ORDER TO WRITE. REALITY: YOU OFTEN NEED TO WRITE IN ORDER TO HAVE ANYTHING TO SAY. THOUGHT COMES WITH WRITING, AND WRITING MAY NEVER COME IF IT IS POSTPONED UNTIL WE ARE SATISFIED THAT WE HAVE SOMETHING TO SAY... THE ASSERTION OF WRITE FIRST, SEE WHAT YOU HAD TO SAY LATER APPLIES TO ALL MANIFESTATIONS OF WRITTEN LANGUAGE, TO LETTERS...AS WELL AS TO DIARIES AND JOURNALS"

FRANK SMITH

"SACRED EXPERIENCES GAIN VALIDITY BY BEING RECORDED...AND SEEN OVER A PERIOD OF YEARS, A LIFE RECORDED DAY BY DAY AND PAGE BY PAGE ASSUMES PATTERN AND PURPOSE. A JOURNAL THUS BECOMES A VEHICLE FOR SEEING GOD'S INTERACTION WITH US."

JANET BRIGHAM

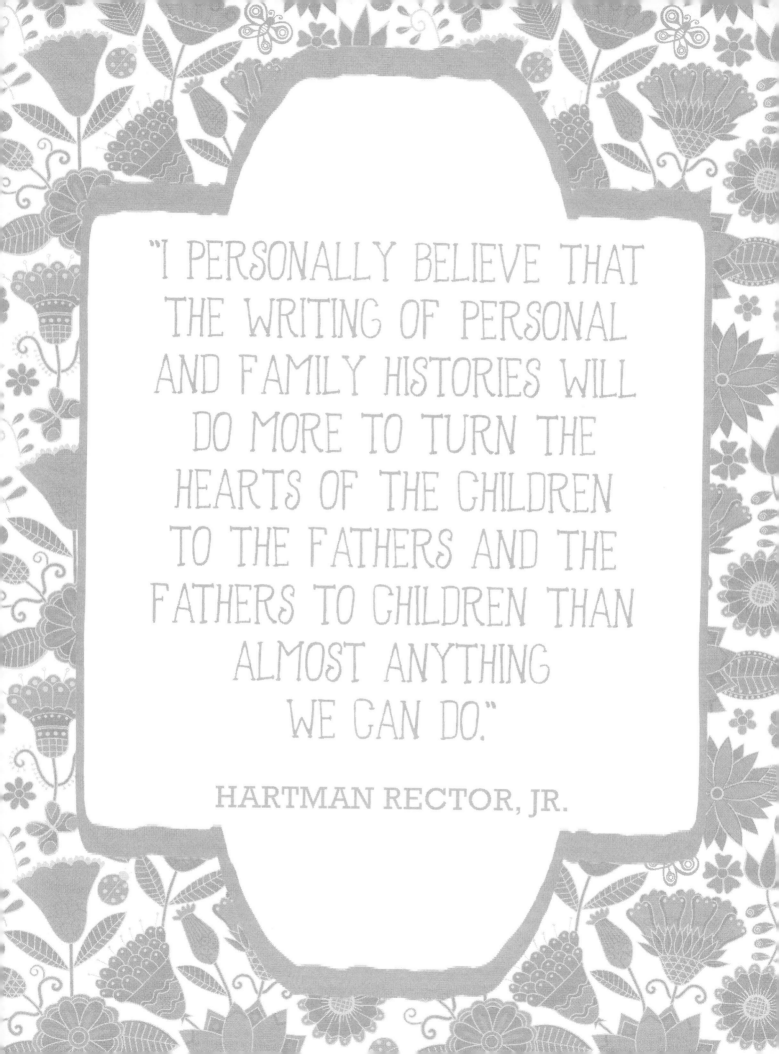

"I PERSONALLY BELIEVE THAT THE WRITING OF PERSONAL AND FAMILY HISTORIES WILL DO MORE TO TURN THE HEARTS OF THE CHILDREN TO THE FATHERS AND THE FATHERS TO CHILDREN THAN ALMOST ANYTHING WE CAN DO."

HARTMAN RECTOR, JR.

"I HAVEN'T WRITTEN FOR A FEW DAYS, BECAUSE I WANTED FIRST OF ALL TO THINK ABOUT MY DIARY. IT'S AN ODD IDEA FOR SOMEONE LIKE ME TO KEEP A DIARY; NOT ONLY BECAUSE I HAVE NEVER DONE SO BEFORE, BUT BECAUSE IT SEEMS TO ME THAT NEITHER I—NOR FOR THAT MATTER ANYONE ELSE—WILL BE INTERESTED IN THE UNBOSOMINGS OF A THIRTEEN-YEAR-OLD SCHOOLGIRL. STILL, WHAT DOES THAT MATTER? I WANT TO WRITE, BUT MORE THAN THAT, I WANT TO BRING OUT ALL KINDS OF THINGS THAT LIE BURIED DEEP IN MY HEART"

ANNE FRANK

"JOURNALS MAKE IT EASY FOR ME TO LOOK BACK OVER MY OWN LIFE AND SEE THE PROGRESS I AM—OR AM NOT—MAKING. THEY CAN MOTIVATE ME TO STAY ON COURSE OR MAKE POSITIVE CHANGES."

BRAD WILCOX

"DON'T TRUST YOUR MEMORY, JOT IT ALL DOWN."

EARL SCHOAFF

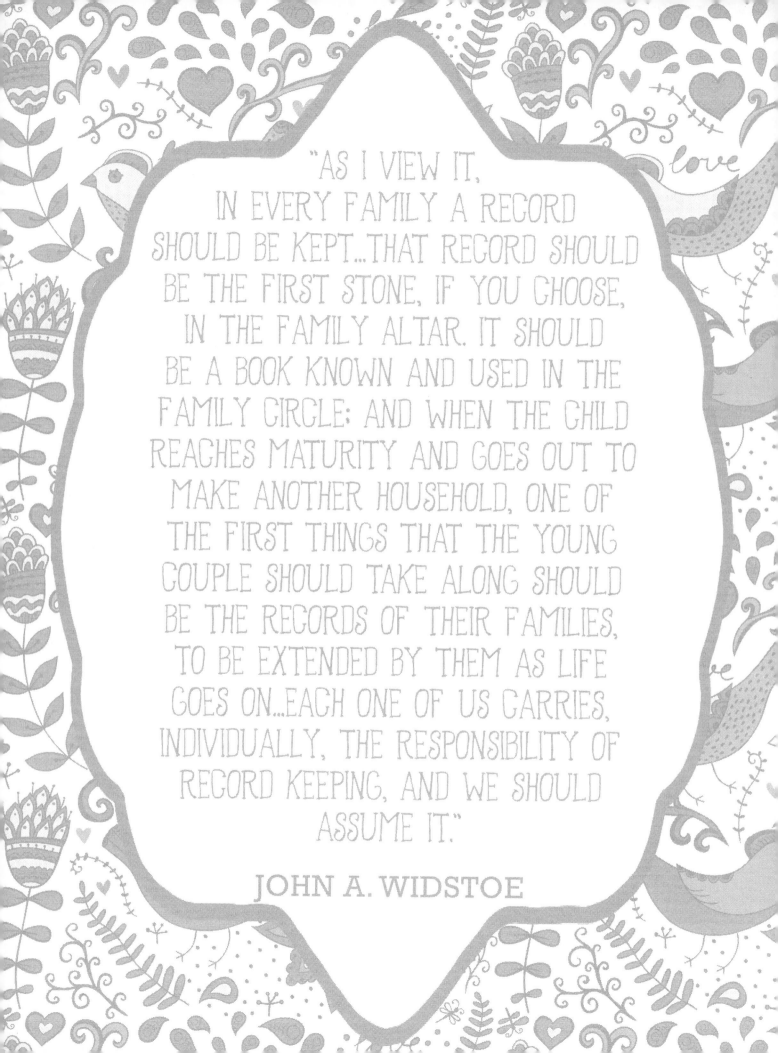

"AS I VIEW IT,
IN EVERY FAMILY A RECORD
SHOULD BE KEPT...THAT RECORD SHOULD
BE THE FIRST STONE, IF YOU CHOOSE,
IN THE FAMILY ALTAR. IT SHOULD
BE A BOOK KNOWN AND USED IN THE
FAMILY CIRCLE; AND WHEN THE CHILD
REACHES MATURITY AND GOES OUT TO
MAKE ANOTHER HOUSEHOLD, ONE OF
THE FIRST THINGS THAT THE YOUNG
COUPLE SHOULD TAKE ALONG SHOULD
BE THE RECORDS OF THEIR FAMILIES,
TO BE EXTENDED BY THEM AS LIFE
GOES ON...EACH ONE OF US CARRIES,
INDIVIDUALLY, THE RESPONSIBILITY OF
RECORD KEEPING, AND WE SHOULD
ASSUME IT."

JOHN A. WIDSTOE

"NEVER FORGET THAT WRITING IS AS CLOSE AS WE GET TO KEEPING A HOLD ON THE THOUSAND AND ONE THINGS—CHILDHOOD, CERTAINTIES, CITIES, DOUBTS, DREAMS, INSTANTS, PHRASES, PARENTS, LOVES—THAT GO ON SLIPPING LIKE SAND THROUGH OUR FINGERS."

SALMAN RUSHDIE

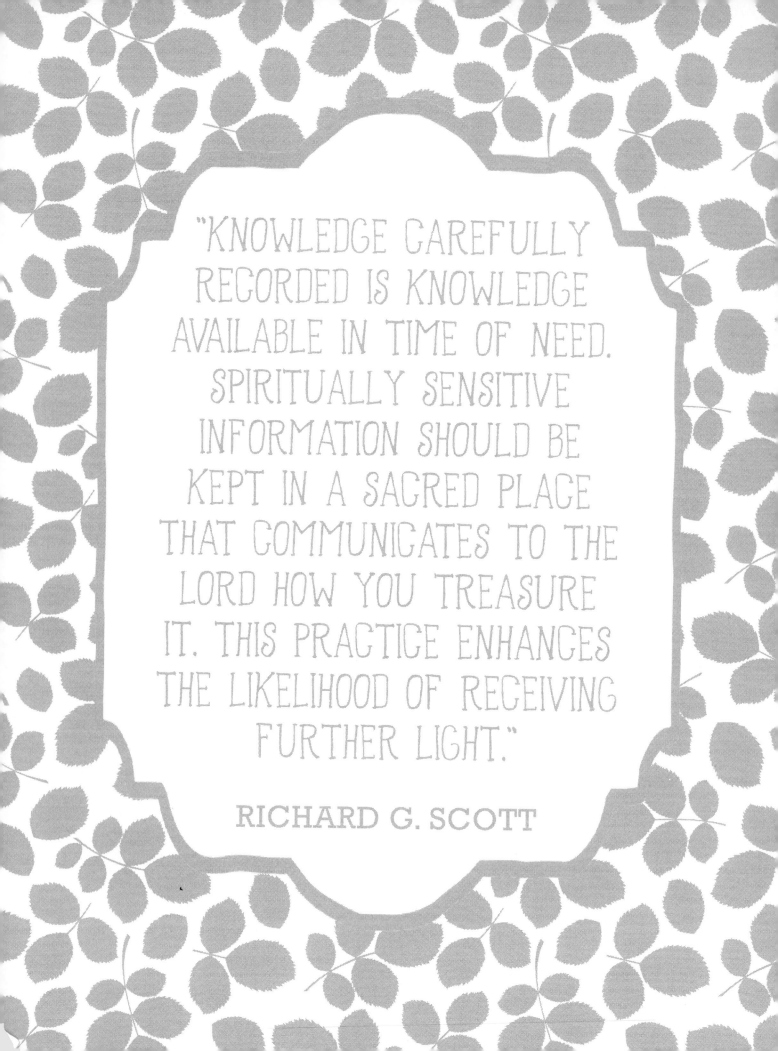

"KNOWLEDGE CAREFULLY RECORDED IS KNOWLEDGE AVAILABLE IN TIME OF NEED. SPIRITUALLY SENSITIVE INFORMATION SHOULD BE KEPT IN A SACRED PLACE THAT COMMUNICATES TO THE LORD HOW YOU TREASURE IT. THIS PRACTICE ENHANCES THE LIKELIHOOD OF RECEIVING FURTHER LIGHT."

RICHARD G. SCOTT

"PRESERVE YOUR MEMORIES, KEEP THEM WELL, WHAT YOU FORGET YOU CAN NEVER RETELL."

LOUISA MAY ALCOTT

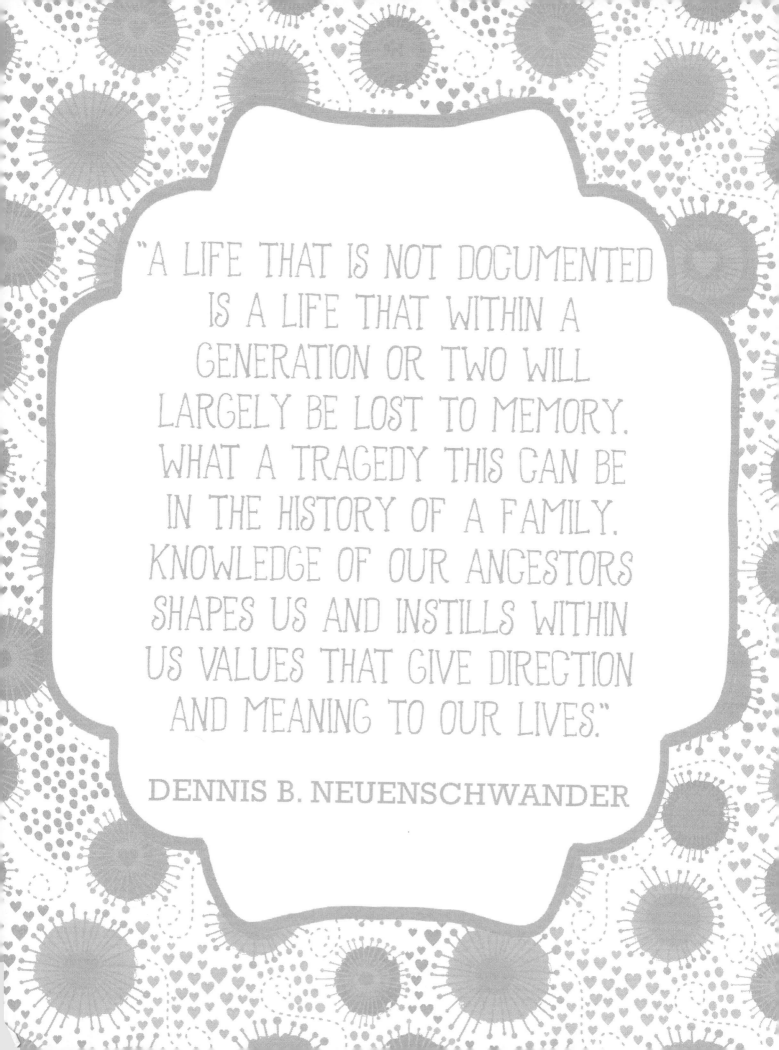

"A LIFE THAT IS NOT DOCUMENTED IS A LIFE THAT WITHIN A GENERATION OR TWO WILL LARGELY BE LOST TO MEMORY. WHAT A TRAGEDY THIS CAN BE IN THE HISTORY OF A FAMILY. KNOWLEDGE OF OUR ANCESTORS SHAPES US AND INSTILLS WITHIN US VALUES THAT GIVE DIRECTION AND MEANING TO OUR LIVES."

DENNIS B. NEUENSCHWANDER

"DON'T FORGET —
NO ONE ELSE SEES THE
WORLD THE WAY YOU
DO, SO NO ONE ELSE CAN
TELL THE STORIES THAT
YOU HAVE TO TELL."

CHARLES DE LINT

"WHEN OUR CHILDREN WERE VERY SMALL, I STARTED TO WRITE DOWN A FEW THINGS ABOUT WHAT HAPPENED EVERY DAY... I WROTE DOWN A FEW LINES EVERY DAY FOR YEARS. I NEVER MISSED A DAY NO MATTER HOW TIRED I WAS OR HOW EARLY I WOULD HAVE TO START THE NEXT DAY. BEFORE I WOULD WRITE, I WOULD PONDER THIS QUESTION: 'HAVE I SEEN THE HAND OF GOD REACHING OUT TO TOUCH US OR OUR CHILDREN OR OUR FAMILY TODAY?' AS I KEPT AT IT, SOMETHING BEGAN TO HAPPEN. AS I WOULD CAST MY MIND OVER THE DAY, I WOULD SEE EVIDENCE OF WHAT GOD HAD DONE FOR ONE OF US THAT I HAD NOT RECOGNIZED IN THE BUSY MOMENTS OF THE DAY. AS THAT HAPPENED, AND IT HAPPENED OFTEN, I REALIZED THAT TRYING TO REMEMBER HAD ALLOWED GOD TO SHOW ME WHAT HE HAD DONE.

"YOU MAY NOT KEEP A JOURNAL. YOU MAY NOT SHARE WHATEVER RECORD YOU KEEP WITH THOSE YOU LOVE AND SERVE. BUT YOU AND THEY WILL BE BLESSED AS YOU REMEMBER WHAT THE LORD HAS DONE."

HENRY B. EYRING

"TREAT THE PAST
AS A SCHOOL."

JIM ROHN

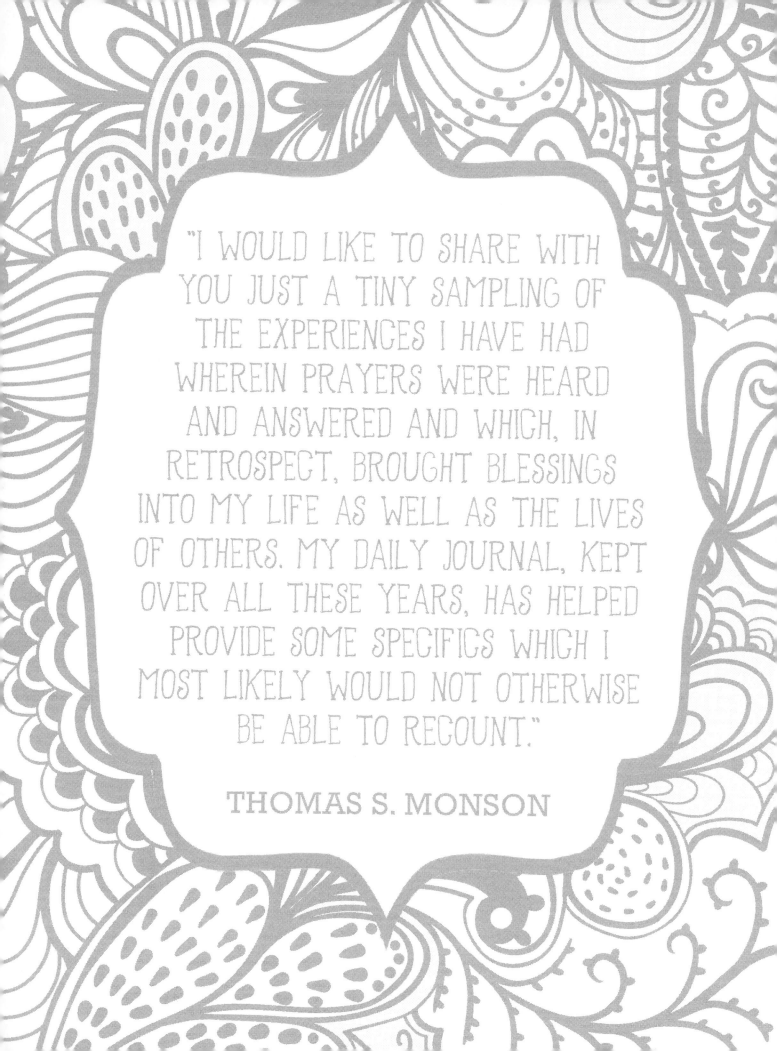

"I WOULD LIKE TO SHARE WITH YOU JUST A TINY SAMPLING OF THE EXPERIENCES I HAVE HAD WHEREIN PRAYERS WERE HEARD AND ANSWERED AND WHICH, IN RETROSPECT, BROUGHT BLESSINGS INTO MY LIFE AS WELL AS THE LIVES OF OTHERS. MY DAILY JOURNAL, KEPT OVER ALL THESE YEARS, HAS HELPED PROVIDE SOME SPECIFICS WHICH I MOST LIKELY WOULD NOT OTHERWISE BE ABLE TO RECOUNT."

THOMAS S. MONSON

BE SURE TO FOLLOW US
ON SOCIAL MEDIA FOR THE
LATEST NEWS, SNEAK
PEEKS, & GIVEAWAYS

📷 @PapeterieBleu

f Papeterie Bleu

🐦 @PapeterieBleu

ADD YOURSELF TO OUR MONTHLY
NEWSLETTER FOR FREE DIGITAL
DOWNLOADS AND DISCOUNT CODES

www.papeteriebleu.com/newsletter

CHECK OUT OUR OTHER BOOKS!

www.papeteriebleu.com

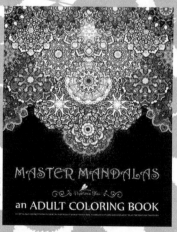

CHECK OUT OUR OTHER BOOKS!

www.papeteriebleu.com

Sugar SKULLS at MIDNIGHT

an ADULT COLORING BOOK

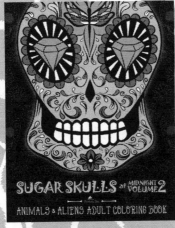

SUGAR SKULLS at MIDNIGHT VOLUME 2

ANIMALS & ALIENS ADULT COLORING BOOK

DÍA DE LOS MUERTOS

MIDNIGHT EDITION

SUGAR SKULL COLORING BOOK

DÍA DE LOS PERROS

MIDNIGHT EDITION

DOG SUGAR SKULL COLORING BOOK

MANDALAS AT MIDNIGHT

an ADULT COLORING BOOK

EVERYONE IS THE WORST

MORE MANDALAS?!? UGH.

MIDNIGHT EDITION

A SNARKY MANDALA COLORING BOOK

UGH. I CAN'T EVEN.

MANDALAS? MEH.

MIDNIGHT EDITION

A SNARKY MANDALA COLORING BOOK

HATERS GONNA HATE

MANDALAS? AGAIN?!? SMH.

MIDNIGHT EDITION

A SNARKY MANDALA COLORING BOOK

WONDERLAND at MIDNIGHT

WONDERLAND at MIDNIGHT 2

A FANTASY ADULT COLORING BOOK

CHECK OUT OUR OTHER BOOKS!

www.papeteriebleu.com

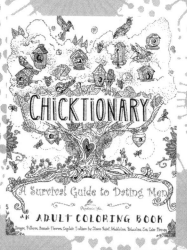

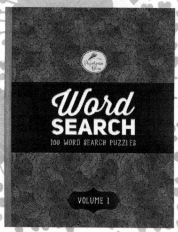

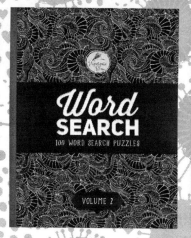

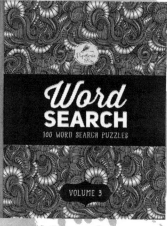

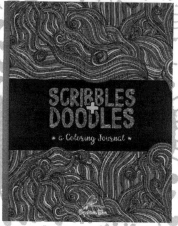

Made in the USA
Middletown, DE
19 June 2017